Multiple Measures

CORWIN
PRESS

The Corwin Press logo—a raven striding across an open book—represents the happy union of courage and learning. We are a professional-level publisher of books and journals for K-12 educators, and we are committed to creating and providing resources that embody these qualities. Corwin's motto is "Success for All Learners."

Multiple Measures

Accurate Ways to Assess Student Achievement

Joan Ardovino

John Hollingsworth

Silvia Ybarra

T 76428

CORWIN PRESS, INC.
A Sage Publications Company
Thousand Oaks, California

For information:

Corwin Press, Inc.
A Sage Publications Company
2455 Teller Road
Thousand Oaks, California 91320
E-mail: order@corwinpress.com

Sage Publications Ltd.
6 Bonhill Street
London EC2A 4PU
United Kingdom

Sage Publications India Pvt. Ltd.
M-32 Market
Greater Kailash I
New Delhi 110 048 India

Printed in the United States of America

Library of Congress Cataloging-in-Publication Data

Ardovino, Joan.
  Multiple measures: Accurate ways to assess student achievement /
Joan Ardovino, John Hollingsworth, Silvia Ybarra.
    p. cm.
  Includes bibliographical references and index.
  ISBN 0-7619-7679-5 (cloth: alk. paper)
  ISBN 0-7619-7680-9 (pbk.: alk. paper)
  1. Examinations. 2. Examinations—Design and construction.
3. Examinations—Validity. 4. Educational tests and measurements
I. Hollingsworth, John, 1949- . II. Ybarra, Silvia. III. Title.

LB3051.A745 2000
371.26'01'3—dc21   00-021527

This book is printed on acid-free paper.

00 01 02 03 04 05 10 9 8 7 6 5 4 3 2 1

Corwin Editorial Assistant: Julia Parnell
Production Editor: Denise Santoyo
Cover Designer: Tracy E. Miller
Indexer: Teri Greenberg

Table of Contents

ABOUT THE AUTHORS

Joan Ardovino has a master's degree in creative writing from California State University, Fresno. She is presently Curriculum Coordinator at McLane High School in Fresno, California. She has been an SB1274 Restructuring Director, an English teacher, a part-time college instructor, a university supervisor of student teachers in English, a mentor teacher, a master teacher, and an English department chairperson. She is a former fellow of the California Literature Project and the San Joaquin Valley Writing Project. She has written seven winning grants and awards and has published numerous newspaper and journal articles, including a column in *California English*.

John Hollingsworth has a bachelor's degree in mechanical engineering from California State University, Los Angeles. A former computer network administrator and programmer, he is a an expert in database design and data collection, manipulation, and presentation. His company, DataWorks Educational Research, performs multiple measures analysis of student achievement for over 400 California schools each year. In addition, DataWorks is evaluating 8 schools under California's Immediate Intervention/Underperforming Schools Program. He has coauthored journal articles on assessment topics and most recently completed a study readjusting the 1998 California norm-referenced SAT9 test results to reflect the effects of socio-economics.

Silvia Ybarra has a doctorate in education from the University of Southern California specializing in curriculum, instruction, and assessment. She is the Assistant Superintendent of Instruction with the Coalinga/Huron Unified School District. She has been a principal and vice principal, an SB1274 Restructuring Director, and a physics and chemistry teacher. She has acted as a presenter to districts throughout California on topics such as the alignment of content standards, instruction, and assessment. As a consultant with DataWorks, she assists districts in the development and implementation of standards-based accountability systems using multiple measures. She has written many winning grants and has published numerous journal articles.

INTRODUCTION

For the past eight years, we have been involved with educational reform in several capacities—as teachers, staff developers, writers, mentors and trainers, data analysts, and administrators. As we experienced the evolution of reform during the nineties, we began to see that accountability held the key to change and we began to focus more and more on this area.

When the federal government began to require states to develop standards-based accountability systems using multiple measures in order to evaluate the effectiveness of compensatory education programs, we helped districts struggling to comply. In response to the increasing need for data gathering, disaggregation, and analysis, we developed a small company, DataWorks Educational Research, to provide support in these endeavors. We have assisted approximately 130 districts, which we refer to as the *Illuminati School District Consortium.*

As we worked with the consortium, it became clear that, despite the mountains of official guidelines, manuals, and workshops provided by various entities, there was yet a need for greater understanding in the following areas:

- Using terminology correctly
- Selecting reliable, valid, and fair measures
- Gathering, disaggregating, and analyzing data
- Understanding the limitations of testing
- Using content standards and aligning them with instruction and assessment
- Limitations of norm-referenced tests
- Including all populations in all assessments

This book is a synthesis and an expansion of the handouts, reports, graphs and charts, and communiqués related to our work. Indeed, all the tables and examples used in this book are derived from real data

1

collected from real schools in the consortium. The book is intended to provide guidance in the areas listed previously. The information is easy to understand, presents viewpoints based on experience, and provides step-by-step explanations, examples, data, and tips on implementation. In addition, it gives readers a concise overall view of important and current issues in education.

Multiple-Measures: Accurate Ways to Assess Student Achievement was engendered by a great deal of frustration and hope. Our frustration derived from our involvement in educational reform. As educators who became more and more convinced of the need for data related to student achievement, we were faced with a huge conundrum. We "knew" that students were learning, but how could we prove growth when there was only one acceptable measure, an end-of-the-year test? Our hope was born of the realization that the use of multiple measures is more than just a compliance issue. It is the only way to measure teaching and learning with accuracy.

We state no claim in having done exhaustive research under rigorous scientific conditions. We simply want to share some of our insights, the general principles, which we have inferred, and the thought-provoking trends which we have observed. For the most part, we have bypassed the political and philosophical layers pertaining to this discussion. Instead, we have taken a pragmatic approach, focusing on what districts and schools need to do and how they can do it. We have emphasized the importance of adopting content standards and developing multiple-measures to answer this quintessential question: How do we know with certainty that our students are learning?

Joan Ardovino
John Hollingsworth
Silvia Ybarra

A MULTIPLE
MEASURE
IMPERATIVE

Over the past few decades, the focus of education has evolved ever more rapidly as we search for solutions to problems which many of us perceive to be crucial. Although it is an area of widely divergent opinions, a good proportion of educators believe that we have failed to prepare vast numbers of students for success.

As the perception of failure gathered strength, the word "accountability" came more and more frequently into play as educators sought answers to the following questions:

- What should students know and be able to do?
- How do we know what and how much students are learning?
- How can we successfully measure the impact of programs such as Title I, the federal government's quintessential improvement program for disadvantaged youth?
- How can we successfully measure the effectiveness of reform efforts?
- How can we differentiate achievement results due to instructional practices from those due to factors such as socio-economic status?
- How do we know which practices to continue and which to eliminate?

Almost without exception, we use a single measure—an end-of-the-year norm-referenced test—as the basis for answering these questions. This simplistic approach begs the question, *"Can a single measure adequately reflect student learning, program effectiveness, and school and district success in their entireties?"*

3

Research on Program Evaluation

The objective of much research has been to evaluate the effectiveness of programs intended to improve academic achievement. The following illustrates some of the disappointing results when one measure is used to assess school programs:

Title I

Despite the plethora of Title I evaluation data regarding the effectiveness of the program, no final conclusions have been reached. A recent meta-analytic study was based on data derived from seventeen previous studies ranging in time from 1966 to 1993. In all cases, a single end-of-the-year norm-referenced test had been utilized as the measure of success. The conclusion of this comprehensive study was that the Title I program had not fulfilled its original objective—to close the achievement gap between at-risk students and their more advantaged peers (Borman and D'Agostino, 1996).

Effective Schools

In recent years, much has been written about "effective schools." These are thought to have particular qualities which coalesce to support high levels of student achievement. In a major study, Zigarelli (1996) correlates the characteristics of effective schools as identified in various literature reviews. He finds that a school is considered to be "effective" when the following variables are present:
- Mastery of the course material is the cultural norm.
- Students place a high priority on learning.
- Principals are empowered to hire and fire teachers.

The 16,842 students who participated in the student achievement portion of the study completed Educational Testing Service-designed achievement tests in the areas of reading comprehension, mathematics, science, and history/citizenship/geography. In the final analysis, Zigarelli finds that effects on student achievement seem to be more a function of student and family variables than of those related to schooling and that the greatest influences on student achievement levels are often beyond the control of the teacher or the school. Again, the conclusions are based on one norm-referenced test.

In a study of twenty elementary schools in North Carolina, Prince and Taylor (1995) find that changes in test scores for the state-adopted California Achievement Test (CAT) over a two-year period had no connection to the presence of "effective schools correlates." Qualities focused upon in this particular study include an orderly atmosphere, principals who monitor student progress, teachers who accept responsibility for instructional effectiveness, clear goals and learning objectives, and principals who are strong leaders and managers of instruction.

The authors caution that, although in North Carolina and in many other states, the CAT carries great weight in school accountability standards and in the formation of public opinion regarding effectiveness, it is not a comprehensive indicator of student achievement. Student achievement, they say, is too complex to be fairly captured by any one method, let alone a standardized, norm-referenced, group-administered test.

State Educational Reform

Concern about poor academic achievement has galvanized numerous states to change their educational structures. Such is the case in Kentucky. In 1990, the state changed to an accountability system based on one end-of-the-year test aligned with state standards. At schools which do poorly, teachers can be fired and "distinguished educators" brought in to assist teachers and administrators in bringing the school up to speed.

In 1996, Brown Middle School was among nine schools declared a school "in crisis" by the Kentucky State Department of Education. Among middle school students, those at Brown had scored highest in the county and seventh in the state on the 1995-96 state achievement test. However, the school fell five points below its goal on the accountability index, thus moving it into "crisis" status. This caused a turmoil among the faculty and staff, members of which had been working very hard in order to improve student achievement and had been feeling successful.

Teachers at Brown insist that they are not reluctant to improve. They *do*, however, object to an accountability system that depends entirely on one test, which might not accurately measure how well they teach or what their students learn (Holland, 1997).

Theodore R. Sizer, author and professor of education at Brown University in Providence, shares this concern. Sizer, the driving force behind the Coalition of Essential Schools movement to which Brown Middle School belongs, cautions:

> I hope we can resist the newly discovered old Progressive trick of imposed, systematic "reform," where "success" is measured primarily, even exclusively, by one sort or another of standardized test, where the route to high "scores" is wholly orchestrated from outside the school and where the work of a child and of a school is ultimately judged on the basis of such profoundly limited scores. (p. 10)

Restructuring

Across the nation, the "restructuring" movement of the early nineties took on a fervor almost without parallel in the history of education. Educators as well as the public at large could no longer ignore the challenges facing America's youth and the added difficulties faced by the disadvantaged, a growing proportion of the population. Restructuring was seen as a possible answer.

Faculties and staffs at restructuring schools were urged to be innovative, to take risks, to break away from outmoded pedagogy. Yet all efforts were judged according to the age-old method—norm-referenced tests—which revealed few, if any, clear-cut successes. Most reformers readily admit to having made mistakes in both planning and implementation. However, they are angered at the willingness of those who oversaw them to make inferences based on such narrow evidence.

Evaluating the Effectiveness of Reform at a Restructured High School

Two of the three authors were among the faculty and staff who worked on reform at Roosevelt High School, an inner-city school in Fresno, California. In 1992, Roosevelt was the recipient of a California SB1274 restructuring grant. Among our many interventions was a school organization based upon the "schools within a school" concept. One of the "mini-schools"—EARTH (Environmental Academy Roosevelt Thematic High)—was based off-campus. Its student population was primarily poor and Hispanic. Because of its small size and isolation and its higher proportion of faculty buy-in due to its experimental nature, there was more freedom to carry out our chosen innovations.

EARTH's multiple interventions included thematic and interdisciplinary instruction, diversification of instructional practices, and use of performance-based assessments. In addition, we offered extended class periods; access to technology for staff, parents, and students; field-trips throughout the state; extended learning opportunities for students who needed extra help; and the same four-year schedule of college preparatory classes for all students.

In the evaluation of program effectiveness, student outcomes were measured by means of one norm-referenced test—the Iowa Test of Academic Skills (ITAS)—at the end of the school year, and results were compared to test scores of a control group at the main campus. To our great disappointment, there were no significant differences in student achievement between the two groups. Even more dismaying was the fact that EARTH's students were not found to have made any growth in their ITAS scores.

As part of the restructuring experiment, Roosevelt had been encouraged to utilize authentic assessment. At EARTH, we incorporated portfolios, projects, and performances as part of our assessment plan. All along we saw strong evidence of student learning, which seemed to be refuted by the norm-referenced test.

EARTH was abolished in 1995, but we tracked the success of our former students. Ultimately, we found that they had a much higher high-school graduation rate than students at the main campus, and so we can surmise that our efforts were not in vain. Clearly the assessment method was flawed.

The Mismeasurement of Student Achievement

Such negative experiences are extremely discouraging since they fuel the movement to disband programs and do away with potentially fruitful activities. They do, however, provide educators with an opportunity to engage in a frank discussion about the wisdom of determining outcomes based on one test at the end of the year while ignoring all the other quantifiable indicators that could be used to determine if students, especially those from low socio-economic backgrounds, are learning.

Such a conversation *must* begin with the premise that one test is inadequate to serve as the sole or even primary basis for important educational decisions because dependence on one test results in the mismeasurement of ALL the learning that should be taking place in our schools.

The following table illustrates how writing and problem solving, for example, *should* be measured and how they typically *are* measured.

The Measurement of Student Achievement			
TEACHING OBJECTIVE	INSTRUCTIONAL PROCESSES	HOW *SHOULD* STUDENT SUCCESS BE MEASURED?	HOW *IS* STUDENT SUCCESS MEASURED?
WRITING	1. WRITING PROCESS 2. "SEVEN INTELLIGENCES" 3. WRITING TO PROMPTS 4. INTERDISCIPLINARY UNITS	A WRITING SAMPLE WHICH USES A RUBRIC AND IS GRADED BY TRAINED EVALUATORS	NORM-REFERENCED TEST
PROBLEM SOLVING	1. OPEN-ENDED PROBLEMS 2. GROUP WORK 3. HEURISTICS (PROBLEM SOLVING PROCESSES) AND NOT ALGORITHMS (FORMULAS) 4. THEMATIC CURRICULUM AND INSTRUCTION	QUIZZES AND TEACHER-MADE TESTS, WHICH INCLUDE OPEN-ENDED ESSAY QUESTIONS, PROJECTS, AND PERFORMANCES	NORM-REFERENCED TEST

7

Changing to Multiple Measures

The assertion that we must use multiple measures does not emanate from the disappointment of those whose programs have been canceled or dismantled. Rather it is the refrain of many influential policy-makers and educators across the country, who are beginning to press for changes in accountability systems.

Title I of the new Elementary and Secondary Education Act (ESEA) calls for major changes in student and program assessment. One requirement is the use of multiple, up-to-date measures of student performance, including those which assess problem-solving skills and understanding (Staff, 1996). In California, for example, all school districts are now required to determine if students are meeting grade-level standards by utilizing multiple measures as part of the Coordinated Compliance Review (CCR) process, which determines compliance with state and federal guidelines.

Regarding assessment in general, an 85-member National Forum on Assessment has issued a set of seven principles. Among them is the recommendation that significant decisions about students—such as program placement, promotion, or graduation—should not be determined by any single assessment. Rather, reports about achievement should be made on the basis of ongoing schoolwork and multiple assessments (Lawton, 1995).

Officials at The National Association of State Boards of Education have expressed the opinion that state assessments of student achievement should include consequences for students and schools with poor performances. However, they say that norm-referenced test results should not be the only criterion used to make judgements since, for example, denying a diploma based only on test scores when a student is otherwise qualified to graduate is inherently wrong. "Students who do well in school but perform poorly on the state assessment may be unfairly penalized by a one-shot evaluation of their accumulated school work" (Lawton, 1997).

Additionally, no standardized test should be used as the sole factor in determining which students should enter college. The Scholastic Aptitude Test (SAT) is this nation's oldest, most widely-used college entrance exam. It is also the most commonly misused. The SAT is validated for just one purpose: predicting first-year college grades. Test makers acknowledge that high school grade-point average (GPA) and class rank are the best predictors of first-year grades despite the huge variation among high schools and courses (Staff, 1997). Most colleges and universities use a combination of standardized college entrance exams and GPAs. They use a compensatory system in which a student with a high GPA and a low SAT score can be accepted along with a student who has a high SAT score and a low GPA.

In his commentary "From Multiple Choice to Multiple Choices," Supovitz concludes that any single test is biased because it depends on only one approach to get to the real questions in education: What has the student learned and what does the student know? He also asserts that any

8

student learned and what does the student know? He also asserts that any single testing method has its own particular set of blinders and that *bias is intrinsic in any type of test*. Consequently, the problem of bias cannot be eliminated just by reformulating any one single test (Supovitz and Brennan, 1997).

Supovitz reached his conclusion after examining the relative equity of the standardized test scores and portfolios of primary-grade urban school children. The study concludes that portfolios are more biased in terms of gender, while standardized tests are more biased in terms of race and ethnicity.

These findings are echoed in other research. Investigations have addressed the ways that achievement gains in mathematics and science correspond to the social distribution of family socio-economic status (Smith and Lee, 1996). And scores on national norm-referenced student achievement examinations were found to be highly correlated to inherent qualities, such as IQ, which are independent of teacher influence (Darling-Hammond, 1983).

Multiple Measures: A Better Way to Evaluate Student Achievement

For a moment, reflect, not upon research, but upon your own educational experiences.

- Have you known children who are successful in their class work but who perform poorly on standardized, norm-referenced tests or vice-versa? Limited English Proficient (LEP) students frequently have difficulty with such tests because of the time factor and a lack of mainstream prior knowledge and vocabulary. Both LEP and non-LEP students may develop "test anxiety," in contrast to those who feel invigorated and challenged.

- Have you ever experienced a negative test-taking atmosphere? Some schools see standardized norm-referenced testing as an unnecessary chore, with no connection to the "real" job of teaching and learning. Consequently, the attitude of test givers may be deleterious. In addition, the negative attitudes of some students may affect that of others.

- Have you seen a promising program or activity terminated by policy makers because, based on the results of a single test, it was found to be ineffective in improving student learning despite the fact that there were other indicators of success? It is not uncommon for programs to affect students in a positive way without the improvement being reflected by the norm-referenced test scores.

9

- Have you known students tracked into low-level groups because one test indicated that they were not ready to join the more academically successful peers? This is commonly the scenario for LEP and low-income students.

- Have you ever felt exhilarated or demoralized after reading the publication of test scores? If a district or school is located in an affluent area, the test scores will show that the students are succeeding, and it is either stated or implied that the district or school is doing a wonderful job. On the other hand, if poverty is a strong factor in the district or school, student achievement will doubtless be abysmal, and it will be understood that the district or school has failed. These commonplace scenarios have given rise to a truism: "Give me the socio-economic status of a school, and I can predict your test results."

For too long, schools and educational researchers have depended solely on one measure to determine if programs have been effective in improving academic achievement.

Dependence upon one measure is both puzzling and alarming when one considers that schools generate a quantity of student achievement data, which is a more accurate indicator of success.

The Multiple Measure Imperative

In order to capture a complete and accurate picture of student achievement, schools must utilize a variety of measures when determining the effectiveness of educational interventions and educational programs.

TESTING: GENERAL INFORMATION

Accountability

The word "accountability" resonates across the nation. Relative to education, the concept demands that schools prove their students are attaining the desired knowledge and skills that will enable them to be contributing members of society. Everyone wants to know if education is producing desirable results and who is responsible for its successes and failures.

Accountability means that everyone involved in a student's education has some responsibility for the outcome. It can be defined as the "process by which school districts and states [or other constituents such as parents] attempt to ensure that schools and school systems meet their goals" (Rothman, 1995, p.189).

According to Newmann and King (1997), a school accountability system should include at least four components:

1. Information about the organization's performance (e.g., test scores).
2. Standards for judging the quality or degree of success of organizational performance (e.g., a mean achievement score, which allows for the comparison of schools with similar demographic characteristics).
3. Significant consequences for the organization based upon its success or failure in meeting specified standards (e.g., rewards such as bonuses to teachers and sanctions such as loss of decision-making powers).
4. An agent or constituency that receives information on organizational performance, judges the extent to which standards have been met, and distributes rewards and sanctions (e.g., the state department of education).

In this book, we will concentrate on performance data. Specifically, we will focus on the means by which educational institutions can select, combine, and fully utilize the achievement data collected throughout the year. These multiple measures, which include norm-referenced tests, then become a "no excuses" accountability system as districts overcome the measurement error inherent in utilizing only a once-a-year test.

Insights

In our work as consultants for the Illuminati School District Consortia, we have found that educators in high poverty districts invariably view their schools in the context of the socio-economic level of their students. Although few would disagree that "at risk" students are at a disadvantage when taking norm-referenced tests designed to *rank* students, we warn educators against using socio-economic factors as an all-encompassing excuse for low performance. We often hear, "Our students have low classroom grades because they are poor and a large proportion come from dysfunctional homes." However, many such students *do* achieve, and the job of educators is to find the means to encourage and support that achievement by *all* students.

> COROLLARY:
>
> <u>District and site administrators</u> and <u>teachers</u> must make sure that low socio-economic status does not serve as an excuse for low student performance or lack of quality instruction.

Education—A Culture of Extremes

As the accountability debate rages, we are once again experiencing the "culture of extremes" so prevalent in education. Some educators accept only a standardized norm-referenced test as the measure of student achievement because they believe that other testing methods are unreliable. At the other extreme is the view that standardized norm-referenced tests are invalid because they reduce education to bits of information which often are not aligned to the content taught in the classroom.

Our position is that "no test fits all." Using a *combination* of assessments is the key to achieving the accurate measurement of student learning—a variety which may include grades, various performance assessments, and scores from standardized tests, including those which are norm-referenced. This sentiment is eloquently espoused by Supovitz and Brennan in their article "Mirror, Mirror on the Wall, Which is the Fairest Test of All?" (1997):

Now we are caught on the horns of a real dilemma, for to judge which assessment is actually closer to real student performance, we must know each child's true ability. We have, however, no way of knowing this. In other words, since we do not know the true ability for each student, we do not know which assessment is more biased; that is, which assessment deviates farther from each child's true ability in ways that are associated with child's gender, race/ethnicity, socioeconomic status, and ELD status. Such clairvoyance is beyond the sight of mortal educators. (p. 496)

Understanding Testing

Using multiple-measures to evaluate student achievement poses both challenges and opportunities for educators. The challenges involve the development of skills necessary to select assessments which are technically sound and which authentically reflect each student's learning. The opportunities involve the determination of which assessments measure high-quality learning based upon high-standards. The use of multiple measures thus composes a credible "no excuses" accountability system, one which truly measures all the learning that is taking place in our schools.

Types of Uses

Two types of tests are used in education:
- Norm-referenced tests
- Criterion-referenced tests

Norm-Referenced Tests—NRT

Norm-referenced tests are commonly given at the end of each school year in order to evaluate how well students and student groups are learning as compared to other students and student groups. These tests are usually mandated by a State Department of Education's accountability requirements. Examples include the CAT5, Stanford Achievement Test (SAT9), and Iowa Test of Academic Skills (ITAS).

With percentile scores from 1 to 99, these tests are designed to *rank* students against each other. Technically, the score represents how well a student performed compared to all other students in the same grade taking the same test nationwide. If a student receives a percentile score of 42, for example, then he scored as well as 42% of the student population. A percentile score of 50 represents the "center" of the population. The highest score students can receive is 99 and the lowest a score of 1. These tests are designed to generate a "bell curve" ranking of students.

Norm-Referenced Tests
Are Designed to Produce a Bell-Curve Result

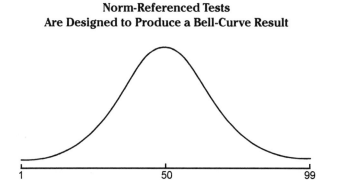

Norm-referenced test results are often used to determine if students should be placed in remedial, average, and advanced classes. The test questions are selected for their ability to rank students, not for how well they match the learning outcomes.

Here is how it works. Every few years, tests are "normed" by the test makers. Questions which *most* students either can or cannot answer are eliminated in order to maintain the normal distribution. In other words, questions which every student can answer are thrown out because the results cannot be used to rank students. Questions that only 50% to 70% of the students can answer are included. In a properly designed and maintained norm referenced test, the overall scores can never be raised because the 50th percentile always represents the average student score.

According to "How A Standardized Achievement Test is Built" (Burrill, undated), one of the first considerations for selecting test questions is to determine what content is being taught across the country. For a math test, for example, Harcourt Brace surveys the content of published math textbook series. For each textbook selected, they measure the "percentage of total pages devoted" to each math topic. Future trends in education such as "new math" are evaluated and questions added to anticipate new curricular directions. Educators and consultants provide additional advice, and then the final list of questions is determined.

When the tests are given, however, the success for individual students is highly influenced by how well the topics selected for the test correspond with the topics their teachers have actually covered in class. If, for example, a math test has questions covering quadratic equations and this is not part of the content standards focused upon in the classroom, the students do poorly. Students who have been taught only "traditional math" or only "new math" can also score poorly. Scores will, therefore, vary according to the alignments of the subject matter selected by the NRT manufacturer to that taught in each class.

Insights

When a district does not rank high in academic achievement as measured by the mandated norm-referenced test, the school board members are often very critical of the superintendent, the superintendent is critical of the principals, and the principals are critical of the teachers. All are admonished: "There should be no excuses for low performance!"

In the media, schools and districts are compared as if the playing fields were level. This leads to the assumption by the public that many educators are not doing a good job—an assumption with many negative ramifications, including lowering of teacher morale.

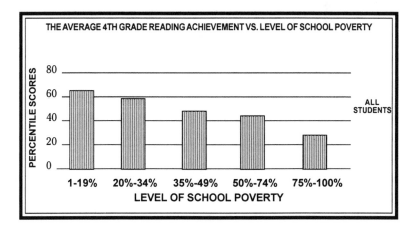

THE AVERAGE 4TH GRADE READING ACHIEVEMENT VS. LEVEL OF SCHOOL POVERTY

Adapted from ABT Associates, *Prospects: The Congressionally Mandated Study of Education Growth and Opportunity Interim Report* (Washington, DC: U. S. Department of Education, 1993), pp. 76-93.

Because we want to ensure a more realistic understanding of why some students fail to achieve, we have spent many hours ascertaining the correlation of socio-economic status to norm-referenced tests.

The foregoing chart shows fourth graders with a mean reading percentile score of 68 when a school has a poverty rate of 1 to 19 %. The scores have dropped to 28 when the poverty rate reaches 75 to 100%. Controlling for socio-economic status, the test scores begin to decline once the percentage of low-income students in a school reaches **30 PERCENT**, and the decline becomes quite dramatic when school poverty reaches 75 percent. This effect is largely due to the misalignment of the norm-referenced tests to classroom instruction causing the tests to be a measure of knowledge learned outside of the classroom. Additionally, in our own analylsis of thousands of pieces of actual student work, it was found that the instruction provided students in low performing schools is often well below grade-level standards. See Chapter 7 for additional information on Curriculum Calibration to state standards.

COROLLARY:

District and site administrators and teachers must be aware of two things:

- **Success or failure may be the result of external conditions.**
- **Outcomes may not truly indicate the quality of a school's instructional program.**

Both statements are especially true when accountability depends solely on an external norm-referenced test.

Criterion-Referenced Tests (CRT)

Criterion-referenced tests measure how well students have mastered a specified set of learning outcomes. Educators at all levels may use this type of test when they want to determine how well students have learned the knowledge and skills they are expected to learn and how well teachers are teaching. There is no attempt to use the scores to rank students.

An example of this test is the eighth-grade United States Constitution Test. Students pass if they obtain a certain number of correct questions. Because it is a criterion-referenced test, it is possible that on a given day *all* students could pass the test if they know the material. This is in direct opposition to a norm-referenced test, in which 50 percent of the students are *always* below average.

Insights

Many districts in the *Illuminati School District Consortium* primarily serve disadvantaged students; consequently, we are continuously asked how to improve academic achievement. Our response is that high quality programs should be developed at the school level. Attempting to improve student rankings on a norm-referenced test is difficult to impossible if the test is not aligned with the curriculum, as is often the case.

COROLLARY:

District and site administrators and teachers must remember that superior accountability systems include assessments at the state, district, and school levels. The assessments that can be more influenced by teachers are the ones that are closest to them. It is therefore imperative that school personnel become experts in the technical aspects of tests.

Standardization of Tests

Both NRTs and CRTs can be standardized. Standardization of tests refers to the processes that must take place to ensure that scores obtained by students can be compared. "A standardized test is one that uses uniform procedures for administration and scoring in order to assure that the results from different people are comparable. Any kind of test—from multiple choice to essay to oral examination—can be

17

standardized if uniform scoring and administration are used" (U.S. Congress, 1992, p. 165).

This concept is so fundamental to good testing practices that it is often overlooked or is associated only with norm-referenced tests. This misunderstanding has been detrimental to districts as they attempt to develop their own tests because most districts have neglected to standardize the conditions under which students take tests.

Insights

We have found that many districts are not careful when it comes to test development and administration. For example, they may not specify the exact number of minutes for a district-wide writing assessment. If the timing *is* specified, it may not be upheld. This creates unequal conditions since some teachers may give students three hours to complete the test and others may allow only 45 minutes. Tests in which the testing and scoring conditions are not standardized cannot be used to compare student performance across a district.

Another big problem is that teachers do not follow instructions when administering the norm-referenced test. Some give the entire battery of tests in one day while others give one test each day until finished. Some give long breaks between tests, and others give short breaks or none at all. Again, unequal conditions are created, which highly compromise the reliability of the test results.

COROLLARY:

District and site administrators and teachers must make sure that tests used for school accountability include clear directions for test administration:

- the number of hours and minutes allowed for students to take the test
- the conditions under which the test must be taken
- quality criteria that delineate how the tests are to be graded

Tests Can Vary In Many Ways

Tests, whether NRT or CRT, can vary in many ways: test questions can be objective or subjective; test activities can be simple or complex; test tasks can be trivial or meaningful; tests can have decontextualized or contextualized content; and tests can include contrived or authentic use of knowledge.

Test Questions Can Be Objective or Subjective

- **Objective questions** have only one correct answer, which students are asked to select or supply. In multiple choice, true-false, and mix-and-match questions, the students are asked to select the answers from a menu of several choices—usually four or five. In fill-in-the-blank or short-response questions, the students are asked to supply the answers. For success to occur, selection-type questions require only recognition of answers or lucky guesses, whereas supply-type questions require recall of information—a more demanding intellectual task. Both types of objective questions can be useful when teachers want to know how much content knowledge the student has acquired.

- **Subjective questions** may have many correct answers, and they allow students to *utilize* knowledge instead of merely selecting or supplying knowledge. Subjective tasks may include writing an essay, creating a diorama, or demonstrating a scientific principle. Alternative assessment methods such as a school-wide writing sample are subjective because they require students to *produce* a response rather than to select one. They measure the more complex learning goals we now hold for students—for example, analyzing the causes of a war instead of memorizing the dates of battle—and promote the kind of instruction needed to help students achieve these goals.

Test Activities Can Be Simple or Complex

- **Simple** activities include recognizing, recalling, and utilizing knowledge. Although such activities have their place, they should never be the end of the learning process. For example an essay which asks the student to list the conditions that led to the Gulf War is asking the student only to *recall* information, not *analyze* it.

- **Complex** activities (Marzano, Pickering, and McTighe, 1993) include comparing, classifying, making inductions and deductions, analyzing errors, creating and analyzing support, analyzing perspectives, and abstracting. Learners need to extend and to refine their basic knowledge by engaging in complex activities. The same essay about the Gulf War may require students to compare the conditions which led to the Vietnam War to those which led to the Gulf War. The comparison engages the learner in an even more complex activity.

19

Test Tasks Can Be Trivial or Meaningful

- **Trivial tasks** include asking students to bubble-in information, to fill in blanks, or to match information—traditional testing methodology. Again, despite their weaknesses, these tests are useful when evaluating how much content the student has learned.
- **Meaningful tasks** (Marzano, Pickering, and McTighe, 1993) such as decision making, investigation, experimental inquiry, problem solving, and invention allow students to exhibit learning most effectively. An example of a meaningful task is one in which students must make decisions on issues such as capital punishment, abortion rights, and toxic waste.

Tests Can Have Decontextualized or Contextualized Content

- **Decontextualized test content** does not originate in the instructional context of the classroom. District and state tests are most often decontextualized because they are developed outside the classroom context in which they will be used. Examples of these tests include the CAT5, SAT9, and ITAS.
- **Contextualized test content,** on the other hand, is that which is developed in alignment with the instructional context of the classroom in which the test will take place.

Tests Can Include Contrived or Authentic Use of Knowledge

- **Contrived use of knowledge** has to do with activities which are far-removed from what students would experience in life outside of school. For example, answering "prescribed" questions from a textbook is something that students would only do in a classroom setting.
- **Authentic use of knowledge** involves tasks which people must do in real life. For example, a person who is planning to buy a new car might want to research the best buy relative to price and gas mileage and maintenance, safety, and repair records.

In recent years, educators have advocated that tests include complex activities, meaningful tasks, and a more authentic use of knowledge. This has given rise to the creation of alternative assessments based on various products and performances. Although they are a wonderful addition to a teacher's assessment "tool box," they are frequently misused. Students may be asked to "perform" activities which they were not taught to do in class. For example, they might be asked to make a presentation which requires the analysis of differing perspectives concerning the Greenhouse Effect. However, they may not have been taught how to make effective presentations, to conduct research, or to analyze perspectives. It is important to remember that testing must inform teachers as to whether or not they were successful in their instruction. Competent teachers do not give objective tests based upon knowledge or skill which has not been taught. Neither should they do so when utilizing an alternative form of assessment.

In summary, tests have differing attributes, which can be used collectively in the design of superior accountability systems. Regardless of a district's choice of tests, it must be remembered that what we want to ascertain is the effect teachers have on student learning and academic growth. Assessment must be a tool for educational improvement, providing information that allows educators to determine which practices result in desired outcomes and which do not.

Gains on what is taught provide information on educational effects that measures of ability alone cannot. Astin (1982) states that "true excellence resides in the ability of the school or college to affect its students favorably, to enhance their intellectual development, and to make a positive difference in their lives" (p. 14).

Insights

When asked to help districts analyze their classroom-level tests, we encountered a dismaying problem: teacher evaluation of student success at learning content varies considerably and is extremely unequal. Here are sample questions, all covering the same content standard:

Content Standard: Students will know the major works of Greek drama.

Test questions can be objective or subjective
  • **Objective**
Who was a Greek dramatist?

a. Socrates	b. Herodotus
c. Caesar	d. Euripides

or
Name a Greek dramatist:_____.

- **Subjective**

Antigone is one of the finest, most moving tragedies ever written. It was very successful when it was first produced in 441 BC. Modern audiences, too, find this play meaningful, particularly the conflict between individual conscience and state policy. Write an essay that explains why this tragedy has been so enduring.

Test activities can be simple or complex
- **Simple**

The Greeks loved a contest, and *Prometheus Bound* is about a contest of will. Explain why this is so.
- **Complex**

Compare Sophocles' and Aeschylus' view of pain as exemplified in some of their greatest tragedies, particularly *Antigone* and *Prometheus Bound*.

Test tasks can be trivial or meaningful
- **Trivial**

From the following list of characteristics, choose the one which best describes Antigone:

a.	happy	b.	vengeful
c.	faithful	d.	jealous

- **Meaningful**

Using the guidelines which are attached, create your own tragedy using the major conflict in Sophocles' *Antigone*. Although both main characters are self-righteous, there is a difference between the two based on the principles by which they live. Antigone chooses to serve the gods, or divine law, while Creon makes the state his top priority. Make sure you use a contemporary problem as your premise.

Tests can include contrived or authentic use of knowledge
- **Contrived use of knowledge**

Read *Antigone* and do the test from the Teacher's Guide
- **Authentic use of knowledge**

Read *Antigone* and compare it with the Pro-Choice and Pro-Life movements. Then write a letter to the Governor, urging him to pass laws according to your conclusion as to whether people should serve divine law or the state.

CROSS

COROLLARY:

Site administrators must be aware of the assessment practices at their schools. This can be ascertained by collecting all tests which are given at the school during one month.

• As a staff development activity, ask teachers to categorize the tests according to the type of questions, types of activities, etc. This exercise gives an excellent indication of the diversity of the assessment practices.

• Utilize each teacher's testing methodology for his or her evaluation.

Teachers should develop "multiple ways" of knowing if students are learning the content presented in class.

Now you know something about various types of tests and how important test choice is. However, for testing to be accurate, there are three crucial test qualities to understand: reliability, validity and fairness. Although you may choose and utilize multiple assessments, if they are not reliable, valid, and fair, you have not produced accurate results. We will discuss these qualities in the next chapter.

TESTING:
RELIABILITY,
VALIDITY,
AND FAIRNESS

In order to accurately ascertain genuine student achievement, it is imperative that school personnel become conversant with some of the most important technical attributes of tests: reliability, validity, and fairness.

Reliability

A test is reliable when a student would receive nearly the same score if he were to retake the test. The score should be the same if a different evaluator scores the test or a different version of the same test is given.

Every score in any measurement has three components: observed score, true score, and error of measurement. Here is the formula:

OBSERVED SCORE = TRUE SCORE + ERROR OF MEASUREMENT

- The **observed score** is the mark the student obtains on a test.
- The **true score** is the mark the student should have gotten on the test. This is a function of what the student actually knows.
- The **error of measurement** is comprised of factors that prevented the student from obtaining his true score. This is a function of test-taking mechanics, such as variations in conditions under which the test was administered, the accuracy and consistency of scorers (raters), and a number of uncontrollable factors such as how well a student feels on the day of the test or how many lucky guesses were made. The error of measurement is also affected by the specific selection and number of questions asked.

The error of measurement can be positive or negative. If it is positive, it favors the student. This might happen when a student makes a lucky guess and the observed score is higher than it should be. If the error of measurement is negative, something has occurred which works against the student. This might happen when a student is not feeling well or is distracted and thus receives a lower score.

The error of measurement can be very high when the number of questions asked is limited since a student's score can swing wildly depending on whether or not he knows the answers to a few specific questions. This can happen, for example, when a writing sample has only one prompt, especially one the student knows nothing about. This error can be reduced by increasing the number of prompts from which a student may select. When assessing writing ability, always be sure the prompt does not require specific content knowledge.

It follows that, in order for evaluators to obtain the most accurate observed score—that which is closest to the true score—the error of measurement must be reduced. Keep in mind that the error of measurement cannot be completely eliminated. Every test will have some error of measurement. **Using multiple measures reduces the error of measurement as the positive and negative errors inherent in each individual assessment tend to offset each other.**

Conditions Which Reduce the Error of Measurement

Two conditions reduce the error of measurement of a test. Steps must be taken to ensure that the test is both standardized and generalizable.

Standardization

In order that a test be standardized, the following must occur:

1. Precise instructions which describe all steps for both test givers and test takers must be written and followed carefully. The conditions under which the test must be administered must also be precisely described. Norm-referenced tests have very specific instructions, which must be followed if districts want to obtain reliable results.

2. Rubrics or performance criteria which clearly specify expectations at several levels must be written and then utilized by everyone evaluating student work.

Rubrics are tools which delineate the expectations related to a task. Typically, there are several performance levels, from very low to superior, and there is a brief description of the expectations at each level. Districts frequently ask how many levels should be used in developing a rubric. Eight levels? Six? Four?

It must be kept in mind that the percent of rater disagreement increases as the number of distinctions increases. Since high stakes accountability systems—those upon which schools are evaluated—require high inter-rater agreement, a lower number of performance levels is more effective. However, using only two or three choices creates variations which are too restrictive, causing raters to start adding pluses and minuses on their evaluations. Having too many levels allows for distinctions which may be too subtle for easy decision making. Four levels is a good compromise, although most writing rubrics use 6 levels.

In addition to enhancing test reliability, rubrics make clear to teachers, parents, and students what is needed to produce quality work. By providing students with well-designed rubrics *before* beginning an assignment, teachers avoid misunderstandings. In addition, students know what is required to produce quality work since the expectations are spelled out in the rubric.

Generalizability

In order that a test be generalized, there must be a sufficient number of questions so that if students do poorly on one item, they will still have an opportunity to demonstrate their knowledge by means of one of the other test items measuring the same knowledge or skill. In other words, students will have ample opportunity to demonstrate their learning.

This maxim is commonly violated when states or districts develop performance assessments. Such assessments are frequently much too short, with as few as three or four questions, problems, or tasks. With only a few questions, the final score can vary widely due to just one response.

To use a simple example, suppose a test is developed to measure student knowledge of the state capitals. If a student knows 45 state capitals and the test only asks for five answers, one of which the student does not know, the student will get 80% on the test instead of the 90% that she should have gotten. On the other hand, a student might know only 30 state capitals but somehow those on the test are the ones he knows or can guess correctly. This student will get 100% instead of the 60% that he should have gotten. This testing situation produces a high error of measurement; the results do not accurately reflect the students' true knowledge of the material.

This case illustrates the statistical problem inherent with a test using a limited number of questions. In the case of the 50 states, of course, a test could ask for all the capitals. However, in most situations, such as a math test, only a finite number of questions are asked from the infinite number of possibilities.

Wiggins says that "unpiloted, one-event testing in the performance area is even more dangerous than one-shot multiple-choice testing, because multiple-choice tests have many different but related items, which makes reliability easier to get and measure" (Brandt, 1992; Feinberg, 1990). He contends that "compared to multiple-choice tests of similar length, written exams more arbitrarily emphasize one topic or another with which a student may (or may not) be familiar" (p. 17).

Standardization of Raters

Rater reliability refers to the degree to which raters agree when assessing a given student's work. Studies have documented that when raters are well-trained and scoring criteria are well-developed, raters can score student work with a high degree of consistency across raters (Hieronymus and Hoover 1987: Shavelson and Baxter 1992). For multiple-choice tests and tests that are graded electronically, this error is very small.

In *A Practical Guide to Alternative Assessment* (Herman, Aschbacher, and Winters, 1992), the authors recommend using the following checklist to ensure that scoring procedures are sound and reliable:

- Documented, field-tested scoring guide
- Clear, concrete criteria
- Annotated examples of all scoring points
- Ample practice and feedback for raters
- Multiple raters with demonstrated agreement prior to scoring
- Retraining when necessary

Conditions Which Support Grading Reliability

Most teachers maintain that they are in the best position to assess their students' learning. This is true if grades can be made consistent throughout a district so the outcomes can be compared throughout a district.

Insights

At the district level, we have encountered a great deal of resistance to using classroom grades for accountability. The consensus of opinion is that grades are too inconsistent since they are based on capricious and idiosyncratic criteria.

Teachers naturally take umbrage. Our response is that there is no better way to measure student achievement. The question is not "*Can* teachers reliably assess their students?" It is "*Do* they reliably assess their students?" If the answer is most often "no," then the more important question is, "How can we ensure that grades become a genuine 'Certification of Student Learning'?" The answer lies in creating the means by which grades are tied to agreed-upon criteria.

COROLLARY:

<u>District administrators</u> must develop a district-level grading policy based strictly upon student learning exclusive of extraneous factors such as behavior. <u>Site administrators</u> must uphold the policy, and <u>teachers</u> must follow it, so that academic achievement can be compared across the district.

Grades are more reliable than norm-referenced tests and other once-a-year tests because they are based upon ongoing assessments throughout the semester and/or school year. By combining the results of many assessments, the error of measurement is reduced. Most teachers have many sources of information about student learning—projects, performances, quizzes, tests, and so on—in order to generate a grade. Thus, the cumulative grade at the end of the marking period is more reliable than any single assessment (Archives, 1996).

The problem with grades is that they are not an accurate measurement of what students know when one or more of the following are true:

- Factors such as attendance and behavior are included.
- It can't be ensured that the work was done entirely by the student, as is the case with out-of-class work or when cooperative learning is utilized.
- Grades are used as a method of reward and punishment for behavior control.

Various studies have documented that many factors unrelated to the actual measurement of student learning are included in teachers' grading practices. Focusing on a district of 150,000 students, Cross and Frary (1996) found that teachers consider many extraneous factors when assigning grades: effort, ability, behavior, conduct, homework, and class participation. That grades reflect a combination of achievement and social factors was noted by sociologist Talcott Parsons (1959):

> . . . we may say that the "high achievers" of the elementary school are both the "bright" pupils, who catch on more easily to their more strictly intellectual tasks, and the more "responsible" pupils, who, "behave well" and on whom the teacher can "count" in her difficult problem of managing her class. (p. 304)

The widespread inaccuracy of grades as indicators of student learning was documented by Austin and McCann (1992). They found that only fifteen of ninety districts for which grading criteria was analyzed had established student performance as the only criteria to be used in determining grades.

The challenge lies in how to make classroom grades accurate so that they can be utilized for accountability. How can variability in grading, which exists even among teachers in the same discipline, be reduced? How can classroom tests become a reliable measure of student achievement?

Insights

We are often asked how districts can ensure that grades will be credible and, hence, can be comparable from school to school. We believe that districts should develop a grading policy that is adhered to by all teachers and which incorporates the following criteria:

- Grades are used to report educational progress toward the attainment of agreed upon knowledge and skills.
- Grades are based upon fixed standards.
- Grades are not based upon factors such as attendance and behavior, which are extraneous to learning.
- Grades are not used as rewards or punishments.
- Homework is not included as part of a grade because it does not measure the students' ultimate learning but rather the process that students are using while learning. In addition, teachers have no control over who actually did the homework.

Validity

Validity refers to the degree to which an assessment task measures
the knowledge and ability it is *supposed* to measure. Assessments require
students to complete one or more tasks. They are valid when they have the
following attributes:

- They are a reflection of knowledge and skill which is related to instruction and not to test-taking ability, memori-
  zation of study guides, etc.
- They engage and motivate students to perform to the best
  of their abilities.
- They are consistent with current educational theory and
  practice.

Most measurement experts agree that overall validity is present
when measured in four areas:

- Content validity exists when the content of a test is aligned
  to what was taught and how it was taught.
- Predictive validity exists when a student's test results can
  be used to predict how well the student will perform on a
  future test covering the same knowledge and skills.
- Concurrent validity exists when a test correlates with another test that is supposed to measure the same knowledge and skills and which is given during the same approximate period of time.
- Consequence validity exists when the same or similar consequences are in store for students as a result of their
  scores on all assessments.

Content Validity

A test is considered valid if it measures what the teacher has covered in class. In other words, a test has high content validity if it is aligned

to what the teacher has taught before the testing period. In science, for example, if about 75% of the test consists of questions about evolution but the teacher only spent about 10% of the time covering evolution, then the test would have very low content validity. This same test would also have low content validity if the teacher utilized lecture only, yet when students took the test they were expected to perform a group laboratory. In each case, instruction did not match the test.

Content validity can be highly compromised when states implement norm-referenced tests *before* adopting content standards. The experience in California is an example. In a letter to State Board of Education President Yvonne W. Larsen dated October 31, 1997, California State Superintendent of Public Instruction Delaine Eastin expresses her concerns:

> When examined against the recommended state standards and existing frameworks and advisories, all the tests submitted were seriously flawed, with the test content falling years below grade level expectations. Almost none of the middle and high school tests have items that align with the grade level standards or focus on the California curriculum. Although these tests provide nationally-normed information, none of them have the rigor, nor the breadth and depth of content, that I hope all of us want for California.

To compound this conundrum, the letter was written on October 31, 1997. The English Language Arts Standards were adopted November 14, 1997, and on December 2, 1997, the State Board of Education gave its tentative approval to a set of radically revised mathematics standards for California students in grades kindergarten through seventh. In California's case the new norm-referenced test, the SAT 9, was selected before the content standards that the test was supposedly measuring.

Insights
California educators who understood the problems delineated in Delaine Eastin's letter have been puzzled and frustrated. This is especially true of district and site administrators and teachers in low socio-economic areas since their students are much more likely to perform poorly on a test of standards which had not been the focus of instruction.

> **COROLLARY:**
>
> In addition to the State-mandated norm–referenced test, which may not be aligned to the state standards, district and site administrators must make sure that teachers are accountable for other measures which are tied to the standards and which they have had an opportunity to teach.
>
> <u>Teachers</u> must remember the following:
>
> - to teach what and how they test and test what and how they teach.
> - to be sure that what is taught and tested is aligned to rigorous standards and is well-articulated throughout the school.
> - to precede testing with instruction. They should not expect students to know how to build a science project or to write a descriptive paragraph if they have not instructed the students in these tasks.
> - to use tests to diagnose, not to indict students. If a teacher gives a test on letter writing and 80% of the students receive a poor score, this means that students need more instruction in how to write good letters. It does *not* mean that they are incapable of writing a good letter.

Predictive Validity

The results of a measurement should be able to predict a student's further success in the areas being measured. Regarding this aspect of validity, a norm-referenced test taken at the end of the school year should be able to predict what type of *grades* a student will earn at school. In our work with the *Illuminati School District Consortium,* we have found that this is not always the case, especially with districts which have many students of low socio-economic status. We have found that some students receive very low scores on norm-referenced tests, yet earn As in their classes or vice-versa. The following chart illustrates this phenomenon:

STUDENT GRADE POINT AVERAGE (GPA) VERSUS TOTAL READING (NP's)

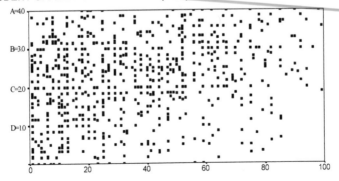

The lack of predictive validity relative to norm-referenced tests and grades is acknowledged by many colleges and universities. This is exemplified by the following information contained in the University of California (1966) booklet, "Introducing the University: 1997/98":

> If your "A-F" GPA is 3.3 or higher, you have met the minimum requirement for admission to the University. If your GPA is below 3.3 but above 2.81, you have met the minimum requirement if you achieve the necessary college entrance test score indicated in the Eligibility Index.

Here is portion of the Eligibility Index (1997-98):

"A-F" GPA	ACT	SAT TOTAL
2.82	36	1600/1590
3.12	21	1030/890
3.29	12	570/490

University personnel know that students who do well on the ACT or the SAT (Scholastic Aptitude Test) will perform well in class. On the other hand, students with good grades will also do well. Therefore, a compensatory multiple-measure accountability system is used to ensure that all capable students are admitted.

Concurrent Validity

Relative to this third aspect of assessment validity, students who perform well at a particular task on one test should perform well on another test that measures the same knowledge and ability and is given during the same approximate period of time. For example, if a norm-referenced reading comprehension test is given at the end of the school year, the student should also be able to demonstrate a similar reading comprehension level in a "running record," which also measures reading comprehension.

If the foregoing is not the case, the two measures might be focusing on different aspects of reading comprehension. Or one test might be a poor measure of reading comprehension even though both are called a "reading" assessment. We have found that students often do well on one test and not on another although both are supposed to be measuring the same thing.

Variations between norm-referenced test scores and classroom grades can be seen on the figures below. Math and language arts assessments were first converted to a 3 point scale to allow comparisons. Often schools assume that they have grade inflation if their grades do not correlate closely with the norm-referenced test. One of the things that should be asked is, "Were both assessments measuring the same thing?" Sometimes tests focus on the same topic but not on the same aspect of the topic. For example, one test might measure basic skills of reading comprehension and the other critical thinking skills. Or, as stated previously, one test might be flawed.

Keep in mind that norm-referenced tests are designed to rank students, whereas grades are a reflection of how much content the student has learned. Conceivable, all students might be declared proficient if they have mastered the material presented by the teacher whereas only 50% of the students can ever score above average on a norm referenced ranking test.

Consequence Validity

This refers to the consequences which are a result of a student's test score. For example, districts may place students who score below a certain cutoff point on a norm-referenced test in a remedial class. These students might have been able to do well in regular classes, yet they were excluded as a consequence of their test results and now receive instruction below their ability.

Conditions That Support Teacher Grade Validity

Teacher grades have the potential of being the most valid measure of student achievement. The caveat to this statement, of course, is that teacher grades must measure student knowledge of rigorous content standards. Teachers' grades then become a "Certification of Student Learning." To attain this ideal, teachers must do the following:

- Understand the discipline they teach.
- Align all measures to high quality content standards.

- Develop multiple assessments for the same standards (essays, demonstrations, multiple-choice, and short- and long-answer questions, etc.)

- Use testing to inform their instructional practices and not to indict students. They should ask themselves if they have taught a concept well enough for students to perform well.

- Be wary of extraneous factors that might get in the way of authentic demonstrations of what students know and can do. A valid assessment does not require knowledge or skills that are irrelevant to what is actually being assessed. Examples of extraneous factors include particular knowledge, talent, ability, or handicap.

Teacher grades should be certificates of what the students have learned in the classroom. For related information, please refer to grading practices in the reliability section.

Fairness and Bias

Fairness means that an assessment should allow for students of both genders and all backgrounds to do equally well. All students should have equal opportunities to demonstrate the skills and knowledge being assessed. The fairness of an assessment is jeopardized if bias exists either in the task or in the rater. Bias is similar to extraneous interference. However, it refers to things that *systematically* affect entire groups of students rather than individuals.

Insights

In one district, we found females consistently outperforming males in their English grades. Upon examination of the teacher-created tests, it was found that a large proportion of performance assessments were being used. As part of these assessments, for example, students were required to produce three-dimensional products that required sewing and craft making, e.g., puppets dressed in historical costumes, Indian fetishes, and the like. Not surprisingly, male students did not perform as well in these projects.

The following graphics illustrate the situation previously described, in which females outperformed males in English class grades. The data from the table has been extrapolated to make a bar graph.

WHAT IS HAPPENING WITH THE ENGLISH GRADE?

GENDER		ENGLISH GRADE	NRT* TOTAL READING	MATH GRADE	NRT* TOTAL MATH
FEMALE	COUNT	246	252	238	252
	MEAN	2.72	2.46	2.34	2.42
MALE	COUNT	258	278	251	279
	MEAN	2.43	2.52	2.27	2.53
TOTAL	COUNT	504	530	489	531
	MEAN	2.57	2.49	2.30	2.48

*NORM-REFERENCED TEST

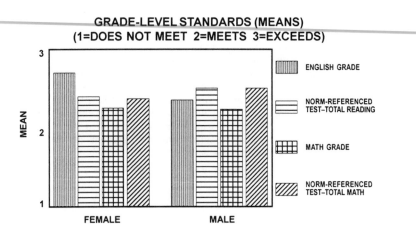

GRADE-LEVEL STANDARDS (MEANS)
(1=DOES NOT MEET 2=MEETS 3=EXCEEDS)

Here are some relevant questions regarding performance assessments such as the puppets:

- Did the teacher *teach* the students how to make these projects? If this was not the case, then the projects were measuring the students' (or more likely their parents') abilities on subjects learned outside of the classroom or the school.
- Did all students have access to the necessary materials? Poor children often cannot afford to purchase items for projects such as these, and others may not have family members who can take them to a store for supplies.
- Were these projects aligned to the English content standards? Teachers often like performance assessments because they pique student interest in a topic. Thus teachers may ignore the fact that the task is not in alignment with the content standards.

In order for a task to be fair, its content, context, and performance expectations should conform to the following description:

- Reflect knowledge, values, and experiences that are equally familiar and appropriate to all students.
- Tap knowledge and skills that all students have had adequate time to acquire in the classroom.
- Be as free as possible of cultural, ethnic, and gender bias.

Testing students from backgrounds different from the culture in which the test was developed magnifies the probability of invalid results (Brescia and Fortune, 1988). Students' lack of the experiences or cognitive structures necessary to respond to certain items is caused both by the mainstream culture and by the setting in which children are reared. The restrictive home environments and life experiences of many students deny them important knowledge of the world. Regarding achievement tests, one should make certain that the following are true:

- All students have been instructionally exposed to the content of the test and have had opportunities to apply this content.
- All students have had experience in taking the test, are test-wise, and are able to understand the test instructions and time requirements.
- Norm-referenced tests have been recently normed with populations similar to the students being assessed.

37

Attitudes, beliefs, and values of which we are often not consciously aware may be reflected in the judgments of raters. For example, a rater's preconceptions about the relative abilities of boys and girls might influence scoring decisions. When evaluating a rater for fairness, consider whether some feature of a student's performance—poor handwriting or spelling, for example—might influence how another, supposedly independent feature is judged—creative writing ability, for example. Other factors which may be reflected in the rater's judgment are a student's gender, ethnic heritage, or socio-economic status. Knowledge of a student's academic track, previous performance, or behavior and the like may also preclude objectivity.

Insights

We have found that the concepts of reliability, validity, and fairness are very difficult for people to grasp. Even after thorough explanations, there is often much confusion. For example, educators at many levels may use the terms interchangeably, or they may understand the "definitions" but not be able to apply them in a practical manner.

One typical outcome is this high school scenario: Students are not allowed to use calculators on the SAT9, but most teachers allow them to do so during instruction. The test is not a valid reflection of what has been taught and learned in the classroom.

COROLLARY:

Teachers must make sure of the following:

- Tests which primarily include objective questions and contain a relatively high number of questions are more reliable than those which are short and primarily subjective. These tests should be used to evaluate how much information students have learned.
- Essay tests and portfolios can be made more reliable if rubrics and precise instructions are developed and utilized so that evaluation is more objective.
- Tests are valid only when they contain questions and tasks based on information and skills that have been taught in the classroom.

VALIDITY, RELIABILITY, AND FAIRNESS				
Types of Questions		Knowledge	Validity	Reliability
One Correct Answer • Multiple Choice • Matching • True-False **More Than One Correct Answer** • Essays • Projects • Portfolios • Performances	Higher Cognitive Tasks ↓	• Recognition • Recall • Utilizing • Production **Activities To Refine and Extend Knowledge:** • Comparing • Classifying • Making Inductions • Making Deductions • Analyzing Errors • Creating and Analyzing Support • Analyzing Perspectives • Abstracting **Tasks That Encourage Meaningful Use of Knowledge:** • Decision Making • Investigation • Experimental Inquiry • Problem Solving • Invention	Teach what and how you test and test what and how you teach. Be sure what is taught is aligned to rigorous standards and well-articulated throughout the school.	Shorter tests are less reliable Must have precise instructions and/or rubrics Longer tests are more reliable

Fairness: Content, context, and performance expectations should reflect knowledge, values, and experiences that are equally familiar and appropriate to all students; tap knowledge and skills that all students have had adequate time to acquire; be as free as possible of cultural, ethnic, and gender stereotypes.

The No Excuses Accountability System

All tests have advantages and disadvantages. By understanding issues concerning reliability, validity, and fairness, educators can become "astute decision-makers" regarding which tests to use in a fair and credible multiple-assessment accountability system. Combining several measures collected throughout the school year produces a more accurate indication of student achievement and provides districts with a better measure of program effectiveness.

Multiple measures allow districts to accurately certify the learning that is taking place in the classroom. As districts develop their own accountability based on reliable, valid, and fair measures, they will create a "no excuses" accountability system.

HOW TO
COMBINE
MULTIPLE
MEASURES

Multiple Measures

Because of the inadequacies of a single measure in evaluating student achievement, a number of state and federal agencies now recommend or require the use of multiple measures. Take, for example, the California State Department of Education's Coordinated Compliance Review (CCR), which assesses school districts regarding compliance with federal mandates when using compensatory funds (Title I, Migrant, etc.). The CCR recently added the requirement that school districts use multiple measures to determine if students are meeting grade-level standards. In order to ascertain whether or not particular groups of students are succeeding, districts are asked to disaggregate the data, breaking student groups into subgroups.

According to the CCR guidelines, school districts are allowed to select their own multiple measures, which may include the following:

1. Teacher evaluation of student work, including grades, running records, checklists, portfolios, etc.

2. District-developed assessments, writing samples, math assessments, criterion-referenced assessments, assessments linked to instructional materials, etc.

3. Standardized tests, publisher's norm-referenced assessments, and other formal assessments (California Department of Education).

Using Multiple Measures to Determine Grade-Level Standards in Language-Arts

Here is an example of the use of multiple measures from the *Illuminati School District Consortium*. Working in collaboration with parents, teachers, and administrators, one of the districts selected the measures in the following table to determine number of students who are not meeting, are meeting, or are exceeding grade-level expectations in language arts:

- Classroom grades
- Norm-referenced test
- District-wide writing sample

DISTRICT "A" ACCOUNTABILITY MODEL
LANGUAGE ARTS

GRADE LEVEL	MEASURE	WEIGHT	DOES NOT MEET GRADE LEVEL (1)	MEETS GRADE LEVEL STANDARDS (2)	EXCEEDS GRADE LEVEL STANDARDS (3)
6th & 7th	Grade English/Literature (F-A)	33.3%	F-D	C-B	A
	Norm-Referenced Test (1-99)	33.3%	1-39 NCEs	40-59 NCEs	60-99 NCEs
	Writing Sample (1-6)	33.3%	1-2	3-4	5-6

NCE = NORMAL CURVE EQUIVALENTS

- According to the district criteria reflected in the table, the following would be true: Students who receive a grade of "A" in English/Literature are considered to be exceeding grade-level standards; those who receive a "B" or "C" are meeting grade-level standards; and those who receive anything less than a "C" are not meeting grade-level standards.

- Students whose norm-referenced test scores fall in the 60 NCEs (National Curve Equivalents) and above range are exceeding grade-level standards; those in the 40 to 59 range are meeting grade-level standards; and those in the 1 to 39 range are not meeting grade-level standards.

- Students scoring 5 or 6 on the writing sample exceeded grade-level standards; those scoring 3 or 4 are meeting grade-level standards; and those scoring below 3 are not meeting grade-level standards.

In order to combine scores, each assessment was converted to one of three common denominators:

1. Does not meet grade-level standards
2. Meets grade-level standards
3. Exceeds grade-level standards

Here are two examples:

Student #1

MEASURE	SCORE	GRADE-LEVEL STANDARDS	COMMON DENOMINATOR
Grade	A	Exceeds	3
Norm-Referenced Test	45 NCEs	Meets	2
Writing Sample	3	Meets	2

Student #2

MEASURE	SCORE	GRADE-LEVEL STANDARDS	COMMON DENOMINATOR
Grade	B	Meets	2
Norm-Referenced Test	38 NCEs	Does Not Meet	1
Writing Sample	3	Meets	2

A matrix must then be developed to ensure consistency when calculating the number of students not meeting, meeting, or exceeding grade-level standards. Using the matrix which follows, both students listed above would have been found to meet grade-level standards.

Three Measures Available

STUDENT NUMBER	MEASURE	MEASURE	MEASURE	GRADE-LEVEL STANDARDS (Avg. of 3 Measures)
1	Exceeds (3)	Exceeds (3)	Exceeds (3)	Exceeds (3)
2	Exceeds (3)	Exceeds (3)	Meets (2)	Exceeds (2.67)
3	Exceeds (3)	Exceeds (3)	Does Not Meet (1)	Meets (2.33)
4	Exceeds (3)	Meets (2)	Meets (2)	Meets (2.33)
5	Exceeds (3)	Meets (2)	Does Not Meet (1)	Meets (2)
6	Meets (2)	Meets (2)	Meets (2)	Meets (2)
7	Meets (2)	Meets (2)	Does Not Meet (1)	Meets (1.67)
8	Meets (2)	Does Not Meet (1)	Does Not Meet (1)	Does Not Meet (1.33)
9	Does Not Meet (1)	Does Not Meet (1)	Does Not Meet (1)	Does Not Meet (1)

There are many variations to this method of combining measures. The only requisite is that the cutoff points are mathematically consistent. Some districts will not accept any combination in which a student does not meet one of the grade-level standards. If this had been the case, Student #2 would not have met grade-level standards. We believe that this approach is anathema to the spirit of using multiple measures—ideally a compensatory system, which allows students to succeed when they are able to exceed or meet grade-level standards in the majority of the measures used.

Multiple Measures in California

The alternative way of combining assessments explained above is different from the one that is mandated by the California State Department of Education (Multiple Measures—Models for Combining Measures to Determine Whether Students Meet Grade-Level Standards, 1998).

Districts may not adapt models to allow lower performance standards than those illustrated. Specifically, benchmark grade-level performance is to be the 50th percentile or higher on the SAT 9 and other NRT; a grade of "C" or better in class grades in reading/language arts or mathematics; and a score of "4" on a typical district writing (or other subject area) assessment with six performance levels. When grade-level performance standards are set for combinations of such measures in a compensatory model, the score on the SAT 9 or other NRT should go no lower than the 30th percentile even when compensated for by superior performance on other measures. Similarly, a student's class grade in the subject area should be no lower than a "C", and a student's performance on a local writing (or other subject area) assessment should be no lower than a "3" (on a 6-point scale) even when such scores are compensated for by superior performance on other measures.

From now on, we will refer to this model as the "California Department of Education (CDE) Model."

Insights

We have many concerns about the CDE method:

- By choosing a cutoff at the 50th percentile on a ranking test (the SAT 9), one-half of all California students will fail to meet grade-level standards regardless of their level of content knowledge. Even when using a combination of measures, the maximum number of students allowed to meet grade-level standards could approach 70% only if all the students scoring between the 30th and 50th percentiles were "A" students. The state's goal of having 90 percent of students meeting grade-level standards is now mathematically impossible.

- The standard error of measurement is too high to use any one measure in a high stakes accountability system. Due to the standard error of measurement inherent in any assessment, the CDE's use of minimum passing scores mis-measures a large number of students since positive and negative errors of measurement in the various assessments cannot offset each other. This is due to the fact that the CDE's formula for combining measures is not symmetrical: AS IT NOW STANDS, A LOW SCORE ON ANY MEASURE AUTOMATICALLY PLACES A STUDENT AS BEING BELOW GRADE-LEVEL STANDARDS, BUT A CORRESPONDINGLY HIGH SCORE ON ANOTHER ASSESSMENT CANNOT RAISE A STUDENT'S SCORE. This can cause the number of students meeting grade-level standards to decrease as additional assessments are added rather than becoming a more accurate measure of student ability.

In the sample below, adding a third measure caused the number of students meeting CDE's grade-level standards to decrease! since any student failing this third assessment does not meet the CDE's conjunctive (must pass all assessments) method even if they pass the first two assessments.

GRADE-LEVEL STANDARDS

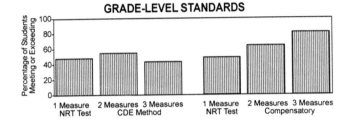

- Students who score low on one measure do not necessarily score low on another. This non-correlation effect is larger for Title I students. The following chart shows the correlation between Title I and non-Title I students' ranking on a norm-referenced math test and their grades in algebra.

PLOT OF TOTAL MATH (NPs) VERSUS ALGEBRA CLASSROOM GPA

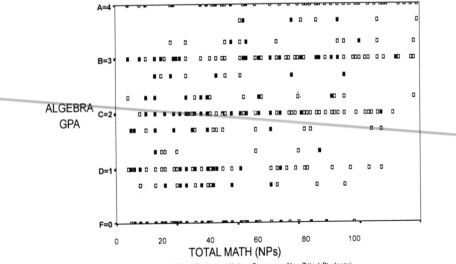

(Solid Squares = Title I Students, Hollow Squares = Non-Title I Students)

The chart emphasizes the effect of using measures with minimum passing scores. With the CDE's system, all students on the upper left quadrant (low NRT test scores with passing grades of A, B, or C) would be eliminated. Also, students in the lower right quadrant (low grades and high NRT ranking) would be eliminated. As can be seen, Title I students (the little squares on the chart) are even more negatively affected.

The purpose of using more than one measure is to reduce the uncertainty of measurement and to increase the accuracy of assessing what a student knows. Various assessments will not necessarily align exactly with each other. Different tests measure different things, a writing sample vs. a multiple-choice test, for example. Also, some tests are designed to rank students while others are designed to measure what the students have learned. If perfect alignment were possible or desirable, multiple-measures would not be necessary.

COROLLARY:

District and site administrators must make sure that the measures that are selected for the accountability matrix meet the following criteria:

- They must be aligned to the content standards that teachers are teaching in the classroom. This is the essence of validity.

- All students must have been given an opportunity to master them. This is the essence of fairness.

- They must be based on many data-points that are collected throughout the year. This is the essence of reliability.

Use of such multiple measure systems may be daunting for school districts because of the large number of calculations that need to be done for every single student. Once the matrix has been developed, however, all the calculations are based on repetitive operations and can be programmed for computer solutions.

After calculations for all the students in a district are completed, the following information can be obtained about the number and percentage of students who do not meet, who meet, or who exceed grade-level standards:

			LANGUAGE ARTS GRADE-LEVEL STANDARDS			
			DO NOT MEET	MEET	EXCEED	TOTAL
GRADE	6	Count	80	96	42	218
		%	36.7%	44.0%	19.3%	100.0%
GRADE	7	Count	92	79	66	237
		%	38.8%	33.3%	27.8%	100.0%
TOTAL		Count	172	175	108	455
		%	37.8%	38.5	23.7%	100.0%

LANGUAGE ARTS GRADE-LEVEL STANDARDS

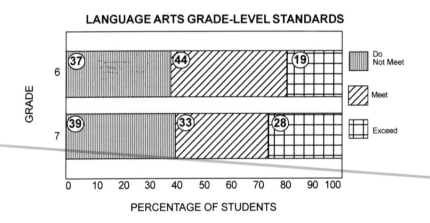

The above results indicate that 37% of sixth-grade students were found not to meet grade-level standards; 44% were found to meet grade-level standards; and 19% were found to exceed grade-level standards. For the seventh grade, 39% were found not to meet grade-level standards; 33% were found to meet grade-level standards; and 28% were found to exceed grade-level standards.

Had results been based solely on norm-referenced tests, the outcome would have been far different, as illustrated in the following chart:

| | | | NRT TOTAL READING GRADE-LEVEL STANDARDS | | | |
			DO NOT MEET	MEET	EXCEED	TOTAL
GRADE	6	Count	99	78	30	207
		%	47.8%	37.7%	14.5%	100.0%
GRADE	7	Count	90	81	53	224
		%	40.2%	36.2%	23.7%	100.0%
TOTAL		Count	189	159	83	431
		%	43.9%	36.9%	19.3%	100.0%

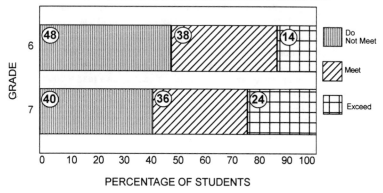

NRT TOTAL READING GRADE-LEVEL STANDARDS

Insights

Regarding assessments and equity, one of the tenets of education is that all students will have the same opportunity to be successful in school. Unfortunately, external assessments and tests can be biased to certain groups because they measure what some students already know when they come to school—their prior knowledge—instead of what the school has taught them.

Using local assessments to measure achievement reduces the achievement gap because these assessments are more closely aligned to what the students are learning in the classrooms; therefore, the local assessments measure the quality of instruction as opposed to what the students have learned outside school.

COROLLARY:

District and site administrators and teachers must make sure that all local assessments are scrutinized for factors that can favor certain students. All educators must be aware of undesirable practices that make local assessments unfair for some students.

- Educators should NOT have students do a project that requires using the Internet if the school does not offer Internet access.

- Educators should NOT have students create projects that require materials that cannot be readily obtained. This practice assesses only whether or not the students (or their parents) were able to get the materials.

- Educators should NOT use only one assessment to ascertain if the students have learned the lesson. For example when teachers use only book reports to assess if students have read a book, they are discriminating against those students who do not know how to write well.

Disaggregating Test Scores

In the past, quality relative to student achievement meant that the top five or ten percent of students achieved high standards, and equity meant that all students had an equal opportunity to participate *if they chose to do so*. An example for both exists when students are tracked. Typically, low-performing students and/or those perceived to be low-performing are scheduled into remedial classes. They may request GATE, Honors, or AP classes, but, for many reasons, this seldom occurs. In the meantime, most of the achievers in the "high ability" classes continue to succeed.

The disaggregation of results into the different subgroup in a school population reveals issues pertaining to quality and equity. "Quality" refers to the evidence that high standards are being met by a large percentage of students in a district. "Equity" refers to the evidence that there is no difference from one group to another in the percent of students meeting or exceeding standards regardless of race, ethnicity, gender, or socio-economic status.

Based on multiple-measures, the next page shows the results obtained when disaggregated data for Title I students is compared to that of non-Title I students.

GRADE-LEVEL STANDARDS USING MULTIPLE MEASURES

| | | LANGUAGE ARTS GRADE-LEVEL STANDARDS | | | |
		DO NOT MEET	MEET	EXCEED	TOTAL
TITLE I	Count	96	46	13	155
	%	61.9%	29.7%	8.4%	100.0%
NON-TITLE I	Count	76	129	95	300
	%	25.3%	43.0%	31.7%	100.0%
TOTAL	Count	172	175	108	455
	%	37.8%	38.5%	23.7%	100.0%

LANGUAGE ARTS GRADE-LEVEL STANDARDS

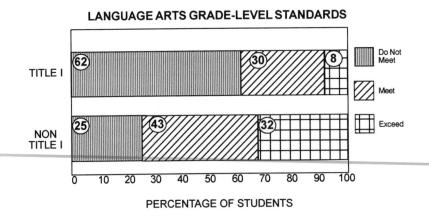

PERCENTAGE OF STUDENTS

The above chart indicates that 61.9% of the Title I students do not meet grade-level standards; 29.7% meet grade-level standards; and 8.4% exceed grade-level standards. For the non-Title I students, 25.3% do not to meet grade-level standards; 43.0% meet grade-level standards; and 31.7% exceed grade-level standards.

Based on a single-measure—a norm-referenced test—the following results are obtained when disaggregated data for Title I students is compared to that of non-Title I students:

GRADE-LEVEL STANDARDS USING NRT ONLY

		TOTAL READING GRADE-LEVEL STANDARDS			
		DO NOT MEET	MEET	EXCEED	TOTAL
TITLE I	Count	109	30	5	144
	%	75.7%	20.8%	3.5%	100.0%
NON-TITLE I	Count	80	129	78	287
	%	27.9%	44.9%	27.2%	100.0%
TOTAL	Count	189	159	83	431
	%	43.9%	36.9%	19.3%	100.0%

TOTAL READING GRADE LEVEL STANDARDS

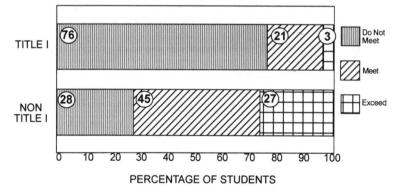

PERCENTAGE OF STUDENTS

According to the table, 75.7% of the Title I students do not meet grade-level standards; 20.8% meet grade-level standards; and 3.5% exceed grade-level standards. For the non-Title I students, 27.9% do not meet grade-level standards; 44.9% meet grade-level standards; and 27.2% exceed grade-level standards.

COMPARING MULTIPLE MEASURES TO A
SINGLE NRT MEASURE

PROGRAM	BASED UPON MULTIPLE MEASURES			BASED UPON ONE-MEASURE NORM-REFERENCED TEST SCORES		
	DO NOT MEET	MEET	EXCEED	DO NOT MEET	MEET	EXCEED
Title I	61.9	29.7	8.4	75.7	20.8	3.5
Non-Title I	25.3	43.0	31.7	27.9	44.9	27.2
Difference	36.6	13.3	23.3	47.8	24.1	23.7

According to the chart, it is clear that the use of multiple measures reduces the number of Title I students not meeting grade-level standards by 13.8% (75.7 minus 61.9); increases the students meeting grade-level standards by 8.9% (29.7 minus 20.8); and increases the students exceeding grade-level standards by 4.9% (8.4 minus 3.5). Although the reduction is not as significant, the trend is also true for non-Title I students.

Further examination shows that the use of multiple measures reduces the gap between Title I and non-Title I students. For students not meeting grade-level standards, the gap is reduced by 11.2% (47.8 minus 36.6); for students meeting grade-level standards, the gap is reduced by 10.8% (24.1 minus 13.3); and for students exceeding grade-level standards, the gap is reduced by .4% (23.7 minus 23.3).

Equity issues can be dealt with more easily when districts develop a system of multiple measures to evaluate student achievement. For the district used in the foregoing examples, multiple measures not only decreased the number of students not meeting grade-level standards, but it also decreased the achievement gap between Title I and non-Title I students.

That's all very well and good, you might say, but doesn't the use of multiple measures weaken the evaluation process? We must emphasize that quality is *not* compromised when this methodology is used. Students found to meet or exceed grade-level standards are those who are successful in two or more measures. It may be that they did well on the norm-referenced test and on the writing sample but not in their grades. Or it may be that they received high grades and writing sample scores but performed poorly on the norm-referenced test. Whatever the combination, the use of multiple measures allows students credit for what they do best. It also tempers the standard error of measurement (explained in Chapter 2). This is predicated, of course, on the use of quality measures.

COROLLARY:

District and site administrators and teachers should use the following principles to select assessments for multiple measures:

- Assessments must measure the culmination of teaching.
- Must approximate what the students are learning in the classroom.
- Assessments must be collected throughout the year so that students have had many different opportunities to show what they have learned.

Comparing Different Measures

Once a district utilizes multiple measures and disaggregates the relevant data, it can make decisions about instructional interventions. Proceeding with our previous example, let us see how Title I students do in all the measures as compared to non-Title I students.

ILLUMINATI SCHOOL DISTRICT – COMPARING MEASURES

		ENGLISH GRADE	WRITING SAMPLE	TOTAL READING (NCE'S)
TITLE I	COUNT	335	322	350
	MEAN	1.636	1.457	1.263
NON-	COUNT	927	731	804
TITLE I	MEAN	2.036	1.986	1.935
Total	COUNT	1262	1053	1154
	Mean	1.929	1.824	1.731

COMPARISON OF MEASURES
(1=DO NOT MEET, 2=MEET, 3=EXCEED)

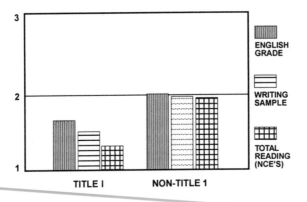

COMPARING MEASURES BETWEEN TITLE I
AND NON-TITLE I STUDENTS

PROGRAM	ENGLISH GRADE	WRITING SAMPLE	TOTAL READING (NCE'S)
Title I	1.636	1.457	1.263
Non-Title I	2.036	1.986	1.935
Difference	.4	.5	.7

Results indicate that the difference between Title I and non-Title I students is .4 for the English grade measure, .5 for the writing sample, and .7 for the norm-referenced test. In this district, Title I students are doing better in their classes but are less successful relative to the norm-referenced test. One possible conclusion is that some students can better demonstrate their success as learners when they are tested with material that is taught in the classroom. The more external the measure, the less well these students were able to perform. This phenomena reinforces the assertion that norm-referenced tests are measuring influences outside the classrooms.

This speaks once again to the equity "maxim," which suggests that all students should be given the same opportunities to learn. Remember that one of the tenets of this book is that "we must teach what we test and test what we teach as long as what we teach is aligned to rigorous standards and is well-articulated throughout the school." The following conclusions may be drawn accordingly:

- Districts are allowed either to adopt state standards or to develop their own, as long as they are equally rigorous. Standards should be adopted or developed at the district level so that all teachers are focusing upon the same material and aligning their grades to the standards.
- Teachers should have a very good understanding of the concepts of reliability and validity when developing assessments.
- Technology should be made accessible to the schools so that information that resides in various databases can be merged and calculations can be made.
- Members of the community, parents, teachers, and students should be involved when the proficiency levels are developed so that there is a shared understanding of expectations.

There is other information to be gleaned from the use of multiple measures:

- It enables districts to demonstrate accountability at several levels: classroom, district, and state.
- It validates the teachers' work. Classroom grades, as long as they are connected to standards, become an important part of the equation. In addition, teachers are the only ones who assess students throughout the year, and so grades can be a more genuine reflection of student achievement.
- It reduces uncertainty. A single measurement at the end of the school year is not a valid way of determining the success of students and the

effectiveness of schools and programs. There are serious risks in drawing conclusions and making recommendations based on a single criterion which fails to consider the overall outcome of the educational process.

Wiggins (1993) cautions against the use of a single measure:

> The American Psychological Association/National Council on Measurement in Education/American Educational Research Association Standards for Educational and Psychological Testing...are unequivocal in this matter. Standard 8.12 states that "in elementary and secondary education, a decision that will have a major impact on a test taken should not automatically be made on the basis of a single test score."

The use of multiple measurements of student achievement accomplishes several things:

- It gives districts more local control. For example, if a district is truly emphasizing writing, the major weight should be the writing sample.
- Student motivation is credited when the GPA is used as one of the measurements. There are many students who do not perform well on norm-referenced tests but who work very hard and who excel in their class work. The use of grades as a measure ensures that they are not penalized.
- When authentic assessment tasks are included as part of a measure, the quality of the content is expanded. For example, a multiple choice test, of which norm-referenced tests are an example, is not the best tool to measure critical thinking skills.
- In some districts, it might serve as a vehicle to reduce the gaps in achievement between the various socio-economic and ethnic groups.

The use of multiple measures offers advantages to everyone concerned. For years, teachers, schools, and districts have complained that traditional tests do not accurately measure what is being taught and do not reflect the many positive things which are occurring. It is time that schools determine the criteria by which they want to be measured.

MULTIPLE MEASURES
AND SPECIAL
POPULATIONS

Accountability Must Include All Students

Accountability for some student populations has been nonexistent or based on compliance "processes." For example, it has been nonexistent for very young children because most school districts do not give them norm-referenced tests or grades. During their first years in school, children move upward without having exhibited any real evidence that they have met grade-level standards.

Other examples include language minority and special needs children. Programs for these students have always been attuned to "process." Are they receiving the mandated services? How are they identified? Have all the necessary forms been signed? As a consequence, schools frequently do not know what these students are learning nor the degree to which their learning "matches" existing standards.

Now, state and federal requirements are mandating an "outcome-oriented" accountability system. Quality and equity issues make it imperative to answer questions such as these:

- How many students in the district are meeting grade-level standards?
- How well are English language minority students and students with special needs achieving and how do they compare to the rest of the school population?
- Retention, are students ready to advance to the next grade?
- How successful are the academic programs?

These questions can only be answered by means of a comprehensive accountability system that is valid and reliable and can be used with all students. If no such accountability system exists, it must be developed. Such a system, in turn, necessitates an understanding of the different student populations and a careful selection of assessments that take into account their diversity.

Assessing the Achievement of Young Children

The National Association for the Education of Young Children (1990) and the National Association of Early Childhood Specialists in State Departments of Education (1990) are only two of the influential professional associations which have issued position statements on how to make assessment an integral part of curriculum and instruction in the early primary grades. They offer guidelines to school personnel who work with young children (Hills, 1997).

- Evaluate current and proposed assessment programs in terms of criteria for quality and fairness.
- Eliminate routine use of norm-referenced tests for all young children.
- Eliminate policies that assign children to extra-year programs on the basis of norm-referenced test scores.
- Make teachers the primary assessor for the children.
- Ensure that teachers have been properly trained in assessing very young children.

Hills (1997) points out that current approaches to assessment stress the centrality of the teacher as the one in the best position to know the day-to-day performance and progress of the child and the one who most needs that information to plan effective instruction.

There are various reasons for assessing even very young students. Among them are the following:

- Ascertaining a child's preparedness to enter a program
- Identifying who may need specialized placement
- Evaluating the appropriateness of teaching programs and teaching strategies
- Evaluating a child's progress

In order that these goals are accomplished, a comprehensive assessment program should include these components:

- Pre- and post- criterion-referenced tests to check for value-added gains.
- Pre- and post- teacher-made tests
- Analysis of student work throughout the year according to a well-defined rubric
- Attainment of acceptable cut-off points of the district's grade-level standards

In our work with the *Illuminati School District Consortium,* we have found that the majority of school districts are not testing young children by means of norm-referenced tests. Instead, they are developing their own

60

multiple measures to determine if students are meeting grade-level standards. In the district shown in the following table, the decision was made to stress reading. Therefore, for language arts grade-level calculations, the reading level is weighted at 70% and the writing level at 30%.

Illuminati School District Consortium
Accountability Model

MEASURES LANGUAGE ARTS	WEIGHT	DO NOT MEET GRADE LEVEL STANDARDS	MEET GRADE LEVEL STANDARDS	EXCEED GRADE LEVEL STANDARDS
KINDERGARTEN				
Reading Level	70%	1	2	3+
Writing Rubric	30%	1-2	3	4
FIRST GRADE				
Reading Level	70%	1-9	10	11+
Writing Rubric	30%	1-2	3	4

The results, after the multiple measures were combined, indicate that 29.2% of kindergarten students did not meet grade-level standards; 31.9% met grade-level standards; and 38.9% exceeded grade-level standards. For students in the first grade, 23.5% did not meet grade-level standards; 24.9% met grade-level standards; and 51.6% exceeded grade-level standards.

The results also indicate that the students attained higher reading levels as they moved from kindergarten to first grade. This observation was made possible because the district used a reading assessment that provides numerically higher reading levels, which indicate how much academic progress students have made.

| | | | LANGUAGE ARTS GRADE-LEVEL STANDARDS | | | |
			DO NOT MEET	MEET	EXCEED	TOTAL
GRADE	K	Count	63	69	84	216
		%	29.2%	31.9%	38.9%	100.0%
GRADE	1	Count	52	55	114	221
		%	23.5%	24.9%	51.6%	100.0%
TOTAL		Count	115	124	198	437
		%	26.3%	28.4%	45.3%	100.0%

LANGUAGE ARTS GRADE LEVEL STANDARDS

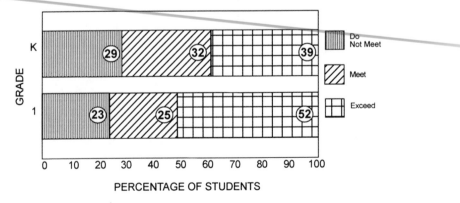

Insights

Assessments to evaluate how well younger students are learning standards vary considerably among districts. Some of the most common measures are as follows:

Kindergarten:
- Letter name identification
- Letter sound identification
- Recognizing/reading sight words
- Written vocabulary
- Concepts of print
- Phonemic awareness/blending
- Independent learning behaviors

First Grade:
- Running records
- Sentence dictation/phonics
- Oral reading/phonics
- Recognizing/reading sight words
- Spelling: first grade words
- Independent learning behaviors

Second Grade:
- Running records
- Recognizing/reading sight words
- Spelling: second-grade words
- Confirmation of predictions
- Location of information
- Identification of story elements
- Independent learning behaviors

Here are some of the more important questions to be asked in these multiple measures accountability systems:

- Is any one measure more important than another in demonstrating proficiency in reading and writing? For example, in kindergarten, is recognizing and reading sightwords more of an indication of proficiency than any one of the other measures?
- Should students be considered non-proficient if they fail any of the measures in the accountability system? For example, if the student fails "concepts of print" but passes "recognizing/reading sight words" and "written vocabulary," should the student be considered proficient or non-proficient?
- Are some of these measures fundamental to the development of later skills? For example, should "letter sound identification" precede "recognizing/reading sight words"? And if this is the case, is the recognition and reading of sight words a better indicator of reading proficiency?

There are a number of resources that offer a wealth of information on how to assess young children. *Practical Aspects of Authentic Assessment: Putting the Pieces Together* (Campbell-Hill and Ruptic, 1994) offers chapters on observing writing and reading growth. Educators in Connecticut's Pomperaugh Regional School District 15 have written a book that contains various samples of rubrics used at the lower elementary grades. These rubrics use happy, neutral, or sad faces to inform the students of the performance levels that they have achieved (Hibbard, Van Wagener, Lewbel, Waterbury-Wyatt, and Shaw, 1996). *The Handbook of Literacy Assessment and Evaluation* (Harp, 1996) contains a whole section with developmental checklists in reading and writing, dialogue journals, holistic scoring of writing, interest inventories, and interviews.

Insights

Small children are very difficult to assess because the results can fluctuate widely from day to day. Another problem is that assessments are often taken too early in the year. Because children are just beginning to learn how to read, write, and compute, these assessments are not useful. To have value for an accountability model, the best assessments for small children fit this description:

- **They are taken at the end of the year. This allows ample time for the children to learn the material.**
- **They measure the desired outcomes and not the intervening processes.**

Students With Disabilities

In the past, students with disabilities were exempted from testing for a variety of reasons. Presently, the impetus to assess students with disabilities has been created by two main forces:

1. The 1997 reauthorization of the Individuals with Disabilities Education Act (IDEA) requires participation by students with disabilities in state assessments.

2. The National Center on Educational Outcomes has recommended that there be one set of content standards for all students. What is important for *some* students to know is important for *all* students to know. The content standards of skills and knowledge required for a trained and informed work force are useful for students of *all* ability levels (Ysseldyke, et al., 1994).

In order to ensure the maximum participation of students with disabilities in assessment programs, accommodations might have to be provided. An accommodation is an alteration in the way curriculum is delivered or the way a test is administered. Accommodation categories are setting, presentation, timing, response, scheduling, and "other."

Decisions about accommodations should be based on what students need in order to learn, and they should be provided with an equal opportunity to show what they know without being hindered by their disability. Whether or not to accommodate should be decided at the individual student level. It is conceivable that some students with disabilities will participate both with and without accommodations.

When accommodations are utilized, it is important that they do not compromise what the test is measuring. This underscores the importance of making sure decision makers know both the purpose of an assessment and the skills or constructs it is trying to measure. The National Center on Educational Outcomes recommends that the following accommodations be used:

TYPES OF ACCOMMODATIONS

SETTING	PRESENTATION
• Administer the test to a small group in a separate location • Administer the test individually in a separate location • Provide special lighting • Provide adaptive or special furniture • Administer the test in a location with minimal distractions	• Provide an audio tape • Increase spacing between items or reduce items per page or line • Provide reading passages with one complete sentence per line • Highlight key words or phrases in directions • Provide cues (e.g., arrows and stop signs) on answer forms. • Secure papers to work area with tape/magnets
TIMING • Allow a flexible schedule • Extend the time allotted to complete the test • Allow frequent breaks during testing	**RESPONSE** • Allow marking of answers in booklet • Tape record responses for later verbatim translation • Allow use of scribe • Provide copying assistance between drafts.
SCHEDULING • Administer the test in several sessions, specifying the duration of each session • Allow subtests to be taken in a different order • Administer the test in the afternoon rather than in the morning, or vice versa	**OTHER** • Prepare special tests • Provide on-task/focusing prompts • Provide any accommodation that a student needs which does not fit under the existing categories

Insights

We have found that the use of accommodations is misunderstood by school personnel. Most teachers think that, in order to accommodate students with disabilities, they must modify the curriculum. For example, when teaching 25 vocabulary words to a class, the teacher might give the students with disabilities only 10. We must keep in mind that all students should meet the same standards. Another problem arises when teachers think accommodating students means modifying the classroom grade. If a student with a disability receives a B in a class, it should be comparable to the grade received by any other student in the classroom Accommodations speak only to the *mechanics* of delivering the curriculum or administering the test.

COROLLARY:

District and site administrators and teachers need to keep two things in mind:

- **The essence of a standards-based accountability system is that all students will learn the standards and not modified standards.**

- **Students can take longer to learn the standards, but the standards are the nonnegotiable outcomes.**

Students in an Alternative System

There are some students who are unable to participate in the assessment system, even if they are provided with accommodations. Typically, these students have more significant disabilities and are not working toward a regular high school diploma. The percentage of such students is quite small—usually less than two percent of the student population.

The National Council of Educational Outcomes (NCEO) has worked with national groups to achieve consensus on broad domains of learning relevant for these special students (Opportunity-to-Learn Standards, 1995). These domains include the following:

- Participation
- Family involvement and accommodation
- Physical health
- Responsibility and independence
- Contribution and citizenship

- Academic and functional literacy
- Personal and social adjustment
- Satisfaction

These can be documented by performance events, tasks, portfolios, teacher and/or parent checklists of student performance, and videotapes and observations of students over time.

Limited English Proficient Students

It has been customary to exempt many Limited English Proficient students from achievement testing because some educators feel that these students are not proficient enough in English to take the test. Lacelle-Peterson and Rivera say that, while this concern for students is laudable, exempting Limited English Proficient students creates a kind of "systemic ignorance" about their progress. Exemption can also create an inaccurate picture of the overall student achievement in a district and make it difficult for educational reform to address the needs of all students (1994, p. 70).

We have found considerable variation from district to district in defining just what "Limited English Proficient" means. An advisory committee convened by the Council of Chief State School Officers (CCSSO) has proposed two definitions:

1. **A fully English-proficient (FEP) student** is able to use English to ask questions, to understand teachers and reading materials, to test ideas, and to challenge what is being asked in the classroom. Four language skills contribute to proficiency:

- Reading—the ability to comprehend and interpret text at the age- and grade-appropriate level.
- Listening—the ability to understand the language of the teacher and instruction, comprehend and extract information, and follow the instructional discourse through which teachers provide information.
- Writing—the ability to produce written text with content and format which fulfills classroom assignments at the age- and grade-appropriate level.
- Speaking—The ability to use oral language appropriately and effectively in learning activities (such as peer tutoring, collaborative learning activities and question answer sessions) within the classroom and in social interactions within the school.

2. **A Limited English Proficient (LEP) student** has a language background other than English and his or her proficiency in English is such that the probability of the student's academic success in an English-only class-

room is below that of an academically successful peer with an English-language background (Council of Chief State School Officers, 1992).

In evaluating programs that serve LEP students, districts must contend with two different questions:
1. How proficient in English is the student?
2. How much content is the student learning?

If the student is not learning, an additional question becomes necessary: How do we know that it is a language issue and not a learning difficulty issue?

How Proficient in English Is the Student?

This question, which is central to the education of English Language Learners must now be asked in terms of an "outcome-based system." In the past, the salient point was that a district was testing students for English proficiency. The most critical point now concerns how fast the students are learning English by the chosen standards.

Which Tests Measure English Proficiency?

A survey conducted by Hopstock et al found that 83% of districts use a language proficiency test in English to determine English proficiency. The English proficiency tests most frequently used to identify, assign, and reclassify LEP students are the Language Assessment Scales (LAS), the Idea Proficiency Test (IPT), the Maculaitis Assessment Program (MAC), the Bilingual Syntax Measure (BSM), the Peabody Picture Vocabulary Test (PPVT), and the Language Assessment Battery (LAB) (Hopstock, Bucaro, Fleischman, Zehler, and Eu, 1993).

These six tests contain major differences in content tested, administration procedures, and conceptualization of the best means of identifying proficiency levels [Zehler, Hopstock, Fleischman, and Greniuk, 1994). Other reviewers have voiced criticisms regarding their validity and reliability, the adequacy of the scoring directions, the limited populations on which test norms are based, and the availability of the conditions needed for administration of the measures (Gillmore and Dickerson, 1979; Haber, 1985; Cziko, 1987).

According to the Council of Chief State School Officers, of all the tests currently on the market, the LAS, LAB, and MAC are most aligned with their recommendations on assessments for LEP students. The Council does not recommend, however, that any one of these tests be used in isolation.

No matter which test a district uses, it must be remembered that language use is an integrated process rather than a composite of discrete skills (Oller, 1992) and the nature of language learning and language use is highly contextualized (McCollum, 1987). Assessments of language proficiency should, therefore, be in the context of meaningful tasks (Bachman, 1990).

How Fast Are Students Learning English?

Many districts with which we have worked have developed standards to measure how fast students are learning English. These standards are usually predicated on the criteria that students need to advance one level a year in order to make adequate progress in learning English. The following chart reflects the typical criteria:

YEAR IN PROGRAM	ENGLISH LANGUAGE DEVELOPMENT (ELD) STAGE	ELD LEVEL (AS DEFINED BY DISTRICT TEST)
1	Pre-Production	A
2	Early Production	B
3	Speech Emergence	C
4	Speech Emergence/Intermediate Fluency	D
5	Intermediate Fluency	E
6	Mastery Level	F

It is important to know that, in order to make a calculation such as this, a district must keep careful records of the dates that the students are tested. The following calculation was only possible because the district had the following data: level of English proficiency when the students first entered the district; yearly ELD levels thereafter; and dates the ELD tests were administered.

Results indicate that 72.6% of the students are advancing one or more levels per year.

ENGLISH LANGUAGE DEVELOPMENT

		BELOW ONE LEVEL PER YEAR	ADVANCING ONE OR MORE LEVELS PER YEAR	Total
LEP	Count	296	786	1082
	%	27.4%	72.6%	100.0%

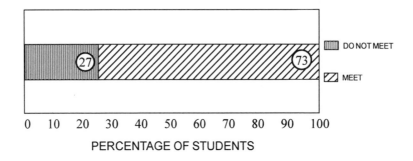

PERCENTAGE OF STUDENTS

How Much *Content* Are LEP Students Learning?

Regarding content, LEP students can be tested in their native languages or in English, depending on their English language proficiency. However, if instruction is occurring in the student's primary language, then achievement testing should also be given in the primary language. If not, the student's academic progress cannot be delineated in an accurate and comprehensive manner.

Nearly all the school districts we work with provide norm-referenced testing in Spanish to their Spanish-speaking students. The following exemplifies one of the districts:

SPANISH STANDARDIZED TEST
READING GRADE-LEVEL STANDARDS

		DO NOT MEET	MEET	TOTAL
LEP	Count	284	98	382
TOTAL	%	74.3%	25.7%	100.0%

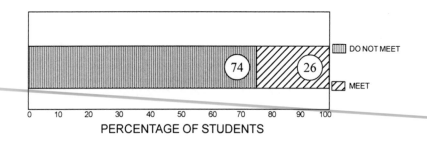

PERCENTAGE OF STUDENTS

The district used the following cutoff values to determine grade-level standards in reading:

- 1-40 NCEs   Does Not Meet Grade-Level Standards
- 41-59 NCEs   Meets Grade-Level Standards
- 60-99 NCEs   Exceeds Grade-Level Standards

As indicated on the table, only 26% of the students evaluated were found to meet grade-level standards. No students were found to exceed grade-level standards.

This scenario in which most of the students were not meeting grade-level standards even when tested in the primary language has been repeated over and over in the districts we have worked with. These results do not necessarily mean districts were unsuccessful with their LEP students. However, they do raise other issues. How comparable are translated versions to the English versions of the same tests? Do the students have oral and literacy fluency in the primary language? Is the primary language the language of instruction?

Achievement testing in English is needed in order to assess how LEP students are doing compared with the English-speaking school population. It must be kept in mind that success in these tests is dependent on two factors: language proficiency and academic knowledge. Hence, the achievement of LEP students is underestimated (LaCelle-Peterson and Rivera, 1994; Secada ,1994). Comparing the test results to the school population is invalid, since the norms are usually based on results obtained with English-speaking populations (LaCelle-Peterson and Rivera, 1994). For the LEP student, the assessment will measure the student's academic achievement and ability to speak English.

In order to determine how well LEP students are doing, educational institutions should use observations and other forms of assessments in addition to norm-referenced tests. The following charts illustrate a norm-referenced test and a writing sample:

STANDARDIZED TEST VERSUS WRITING SAMPLE
(1=DO NOT MEET; 2=MEET; 3=EXCEED)

		TIMED WRITING (1-6) GRADE-LEVEL STANDARDS	STANDARDIZED TEST TOTAL READING GRADE-LEVEL STANDARDS
Non-LEP	Count	5672	4811
	Mean	1.94	1.69
FEP	Count	146	158
	Mean	1.94	1.49
LEP Other	Count	699	514
	Mean	1.64	1.32
LEP Spanish	Count	201	244
	Mean	1.61	1.20
Total	Count	6718	5727
	Mean	1.90	1.63

GRADE-LEVEL STANDARDS (MEANS)
(1=DO NOT MEET; 2=MEET; 3=EXCEED)

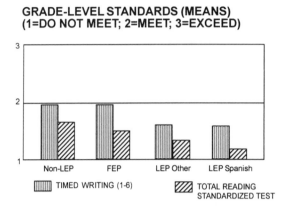

It is clear that the LEP students did better on the writing sample than on the standardized test. We found this almost always to be the case. LEP students do better on the local assessments than on any external test, whether or not this test is in English or in the primary language. The more assessments a district utilizes which are aligned with classroom instruction, the more equitable the assessment system becomes.

Such local assessments are more effective with LEP students because the tests employ strategies that ask students to show what they can do. The following are examples of measures that are well-suited for assessing LEP students (Tannenbaum, 1996):

• NON-VERBAL/NON-WRITTEN ASSESSMENT STRATEGIES

1. **Physical demonstrations.** To express academic concepts without speech, students can point, use gestures, or act out answers. Video cassettes can be used.

2. **Pictorial products.** To elicit content knowledge without requiring students to speak or write, teachers can ask students to produce and manipulate drawings, dioramas, models, graphs, and charts.

3. **K-W-L Charts.** This strategy gives students an opportunity to demonstrate "what I know/what I want to know/what I've learned."

• ORAL ASSESSMENT STRATEGIES

1. **Responses.** Students can respond orally to requests or questions in interview or test form. Audio cassettes can be used.

2. **Performances and presentations.** Students can explain, describe, report, role play, summarize, retell, and paraphrase stories and text materials.

• WRITTEN ASSESSMENT STRATEGIES
1. **Informal responses to classroom activities.** Students can use written logs and journals to record their ideas, feelings, and opinions, and what they have learned. They can also create games, puzzles, and the like to demonstrate knowledge.
2. **Writing assignments.** Students can create structured products such as essays or poems.

Oral assessments should be conducted on an ongoing basis to monitor comprehension and thinking skills.

A Comprehensive Assessment System for All Students

Recent mandates require school districts to have accountability systems which are "outcome-based" rather than compliance-based. Therefore, it is absolutely necessary that assessments fit the following criteria:

- **Comprehensive**. Attempts to assess all that students are learning.
- **Flexible**. Allows students to show what they know by means of multiple measures.
- **Progress-oriented**. Tracks students' progress from year to year, rather than producing only relative scores at one point in time.
- **Student-sensitive**. Brings into the process the expertise of educators who know the needs and learning characteristics of particular students.

All this can come about only when educators develop a true understanding of what it takes to teach and to assess *all* students, including the very young, the disabled, or those whose English is limited.

MULTIPLE
MEASURES AND STANDARDS

The Movement Toward Standards

The recent impetus for the development of national standards was created by the "National Education Goals Panel, comprised of six governors, four members of the president's [George Bush] administration, and four members of the Congress. The goals were intended to set a direction for school districts around the country" (Burden, 1993, p. i). They were adopted in 1990 by President Bush and the nation's governors at the 'Education Summit' in Charlottesville, Virginia, as follows:

- All children in America will start school ready to learn.
- The high school graduation rate will increase to at least 90 percent.
- Testing at four grade levels will demonstrate that students have competence in challenging subject matter, and schools will ensure that all students learn to use their minds well in preparation for responsible citizenship.
- U. S. students will be the first in the world in science and mathematics achievement.
- Every adult American will be literate and will possess the knowledge and skills necessary to compete in a global economy and to exercise the rights and responsibilities of citizenship.
- Every school in America will be free of drugs and violence and will offer a disciplined environment conducive to learning." (p. i)

In 1994, President Bill Clinton signed the Goals 2000: Educate America Act, which added two more goals:

- Increased parent involvement
- Improved teacher education and professional development (p. i)

The Goals 2000 package also included money for states to use for school improvement and a framework for the development of national standards.

Across the country, content area specialists, representatives of professional organizations, and advocates for education heeded the mandate and began to mobilize and strengthen existing efforts to develop content-specific standards. The National Council of Teachers of Mathematics (NCTM) had already been working on content standards and had issued the Curriculum and Evaluation Standards for School Mathematics in 1989.

In 1992, the National Assessment of Educational Progress (NAEP) produced the Language Arts Standards. In the area of writing, NAEP produced the "Description of Writing Achievement Levels-Setting Process and Proposed Achievement Level Definitions," which provides explicit descriptions of basic, proficient, and advanced performances in writing. In 1994, the National Committee on Science Education Standards and Assessment produced content standards which outlined what students should know, understand, and be able to do in natural science.

Most states, with the exception of Iowa and Wisconsin, have identified standards and benchmarks or are in the process of identifying them. Some critics oppose the use of standards while others feel the existing standards don't go far enough.

Standards Defined

There is considerable confusion surrounding standards. In order to continue with our discussion, we need to understand what the word "standards" and the related terminology mean in this context. First, we will discuss several categories: content standards, performance standards, opportunity-to-learn standards, and grade-level standards.

Content Standards

Content standards specify what students should know and be able to do. They are discipline specific. For example, California recently released the final version of its Language Arts Standards, which contains the strands of reading, writing, written and oral English language conventions, and listening and speaking. Each strand has additional categories that further detail what students should be learning All are well-articulated across the years, creating a spiraling effect which, if followed, begins in kindergarten and ends in the twelfth grade. Refer to the following table which details additional categories under reading.

LANGUAGE ARTS - READING

	K	1	2	3	4	5	6	7	8	9/10	11/12
1. WORD ANALYSIS & SYSTEMATIC VOCABULARY DEVELOPMENT											
Concepts about Print	X	X									
Phonemic Awareness	X	X									
Decoding and Word Recognition	X	X	X	X							
Vocabulary and Concept Development	X	X	X	X	X	X	X	X	X	X	X
2. READING COMPREHENSION											
Structural Features of Informational Materials			X	X	X	X	X	X	X	X	X
Comprehension & Analysis of Grade-Level Appropriate Text	X	X	X	X	X	X	X	X	X	X	X
Expository Critique					X	X	X	X	X	X	X
3. LITERACY ANALYSIS & RESPONSE											
Structural Features of Literature	X			X	X	X	X	X	X	X	X
Narrative Analysis of Grade Level Text	X	X	X	X	X	X	X	X	X	X	X
Literary Criticism					X	X	X	X	X	X	X

Performance Standards

Performance standards specify the level and the quality of learning that is considered acceptable and satisfactory. They answer the query, "How good is good enough?" Performance standards provide answers to two questions:

1. To what depth has each student learned the content standards?

2. What degree of quality is considered acceptable?

Performance standards are needed due to the complexity of measuring how well students have learned the content standards.

While working with the *Illuminati School District Consortium,* we asked administrators and teachers how they know if a kindergarten student has mastered the following mathematics content standard:

Content standard: count, recognize, represent, name and order numbers (to 30) using objects.

The answers varied considerably and required various levels of cognitive demands. Here are just a few examples:

- Student can count from 1 to 30.
- Student can take 10 marbles from a jar.
- Student can draw 5 petals on a flower.

As can be seen, it is not enough to adopt content standards. In order to have more than a general and perhaps flawed understanding that a student has learned the information described by a standard, it is imperative to have a very clear description of how well the students have learned the standard. This is inextricably linked to measurement.

Currently, there are demands on schools to train students to apply knowledge as well as to memorize information. This creates a need to expand performance standards so that we can measure the depth of understanding and ability for each related content standard. Each performance standard enables us to answer Question #1 above: "To what depth has each student learned the content standard?" To illustrate, here is an example related to mathematics:

Content Standard: Students will be able to construct appropriate graphs and charts to visually represent numerical information.

If we want to know a student's knowledge of graphs and charts, we can use a traditional multiple-choice test that measures recognition of different graphs and charts and an understanding of their various uses. But if we want to know a student's ability to organize numerical information and to represent it with an appropriate graph or chart, we must develop a performance task that asks students to collect information and then present it in an appropriate graph or chart.

The task is no longer an objective multiple-choice test that can be graded easily. It entails a performance and a product, neither of which can be put on a Scan-tron sheet and graded by machine. It necessitates the development of a rubric which clearly specifies the quality level that a student must attain in order to earn a particular score. The person or persons "grading" the performance or product use the rubric to ascertain the student's depth of understanding and ability. The development of a rubric and its application enable us to answer Question #2: "What degree of quality is considered acceptable?"

Insights

Unfortunately, when states create content standards, they are often pressured to utilize an external test to measure how well the students have learned the standards. In California, this test is the SAT9, which is a nationally norm-referenced, standardized test. The problem with such a test is that it is aligned to an average of the content of various textbooks and standards used across the country. This creates a problem when teachers teach the state standards and then students are tested using a composite of material used nationally.

COROLLARY:

District and site administrators and teachers must keep the following in mind:

- Don't try to align your curriculum to a national norm-referenced test. The material that is covered by this test is too much to teach throughout the school year.

- Always try to teach fewer standards in depth by using state standards which are shorter than national standards. For example, the California State Standards in Language Arts for first grade are only two pages long.

- The best way to know whether students are learning the state content standards is to develop credible local assessments that measure the standards well. For example, if a content standard states that students should write to different domains, the best way to test this is to develop reliable and valid local writing tests.

Opportunities-To-Learn Standards

Opportunities-to-learn standards specify the conditions and resources necessary to give all students an equal chance to meet the performance standards. They were created because of concerns about the fairness of holding students responsible for reaching high academic standards when they have not been provided with opportunities to learn.

On March 31, 1994, President Clinton signed education reform legislation making opportunity-to-learn standards (OTL standards) voluntary. This legislation is known as "Goals 2000: Educate America Act (PL 103-227)."

In Goals 2000, "OTL standards" are defined as "the criteria for, and the basis of assessing the sufficiency or quality of the resources, practices, and conditions necessary at each level of the education system to provide all students with the opportunity to learn the material in voluntary national content standards . . ." (§3(a)(7)). In addition, OTL standards (§213(c)(2)) address the following:

- Curricula, instructional materials, and technologies
- Teacher capability
- Continuous professional development
- Alignment of curriculum, instructional practices, and assessments with content standards
- Safety and security of the learning environment
- Non-discriminatory policies, curricula, and instructional practices
- Other factors that help students receive a fair opportunity to achieve the knowledge and skills in the content standards

Grade-Level Standards

In district accountability systems, grade-level standards are used to measure how many students have learned the content standards at each grade-level. States and districts must ensure that assessments used to define grade-level-standards are linked to content areas and are based on non-biased assessment practices.

One assessment is, of course, not good enough to measure educational outcomes; therefore districts should utilize multiple measures to assess how students are truly doing. A full explanation on how to combine multiple measures to calculate the numbers of students meeting grade-level standards is given in Chapter 3.

Why Standards?

Standards create a template for districts to delineate what should be taught at each grade-level. They provide cohesiveness to the curriculum, present clear expectations for parents on how to judge schools, create equity in education, and provide the means of developing reliable, fair, and valid assessments.

Scattered Curriculum

In a recent article in *Education Week*, Shavelson states that the United States, when compared with its "competitor" nations, lacks a coherent vision of what students should know and be able to do, national standards and testing notwithstanding. The findings from the Third International Mathematics and Science Study (TIMSS) provide strong evidence that, in order for school reform to be effective, the United States must remedy the "splintered curriculum" encountered daily by its students. The TIMSS data should be used to address the lack of focus and dilution of topics in our curriculum and to create alternative visions (1997).

According to Shavelson, there are two major forces that contribute to this "splintered curriculum":

1. Because textbooks are sold and distributed throughout the nation, in order for publishers to sell books and thus make money, the books must contain information that is acceptable to different audiences with different needs. As more and more standards are introduced, the books keep adding more and more information.
2. National exams such as the National Assessment of Educational Progress and the Scholastic Aptitude Test (SAT) test a wide range of material (1997).

Clear Expectations for Parents

Ample evidence indicates that parents do not have the information that they need to make judgments about the effectiveness of local schools. Despite clear indicators that student achievement is low, despite widespread concern, most parents express satisfaction with their children's achievement and the effectiveness of their schools. An international study found the following:

American parents face a number of serious impediments in judging the quality of their children's education. One of the strongest obstacles is the lack of clear external standards.

American elementary schools generally do not provide grades. Instead they offer parents an evaluation of their children's progress made since the last report. Or, the teacher may offer a broad classification such as outstanding, satisfactory, or needs improvement (Education Research Report, 1992).

Create Equity in Education

When students are encouraged to work with challenging content under optimum teaching and learning conditions, they will make far greater progress than those students who receive basic skills instruction (Commission on Chapter I, 1993). Standards that assume all students can learn more and at higher levels guard against the self-fulfilling prophecy of low achievement that low standards produce (Welsh, 1992). When standards are institutionalized across education systems, poor students are given the same opportunities as their more affluent counterparts. Standardization reduces random activities that offer short term appeal but do not help teachers focus on what is important.

Reliable, Valid, and Fair Assessments

As stated in Chapter 2, educators must develop a very good understanding of reliability, validity, and fairness to be able to design credible multiple-measures for accountability systems. An excellent accountability system must incorporate assessments which fit the following description:

• **Reliability.** The assessment is comparable between and among different teachers and schools. This cannot be accomplished unless teachers have a common understanding of the content to be taught at each grade level.

• **Validity.** The assessment is a certification of what was taught and what was learned. Ideally, this is a certification that students are learning the standards because when well-defined standards are lacking, teachers focus on topics that they like or know well. By doing so, teachers fail to capitalize on information the students have previously studied and/or they fail to prepare students for future lessons. A teacher might continue to teach basic math skills at middle school because that is all he feels comfortable with regardless of what the standards might be.

• **Fairness.** The assessment focuses upon knowledge and skill which all students have had an opportunity to master. When there is not an intentional curriculum, the content covered is left to chance. Students attending the same school and in the same grade could be taught very different information. This creates a major problem when districts develop a test because of the variation in coverage among teachers. Not having content standards requires schools to depend entirely on one external test —THE NORM-REFERENCED TEST—to ascertain whether students have learned. Using such tests to measure school effectiveness, poses major problems:

1. They evaluate whether students have learned general information that might not have been covered in the classroom. Virtually nothing is learned about what and how well an individual student knows or can do something. We learn only where the students lie on a normalized bell curve distribution relative to the particular test. If this is the case, the test cannot be used to measure the effectiveness of teachers since this can only be ascertained by de-

termining if teachers taught a specified subject well. In addition, it violates the tenet of test validity: "Teach what and how students are tested and test what and how students are taught."

2. The purpose of a norm-referenced test is to discriminate among the members of a population. One can compare the Olympics to the norm-referenced test. By definition all athletes who compete in the games are world-class athletes; yet when they compete, they are ranked and compared to each other to find out who is the best. The goal is not to find out who can swim or ski well but who can out-perform all the other participants.

3. The NRT is very sensitive to the socio-economic level of students and not to the instructional practices of the teachers; therefore, schools never know whether they are measuring the quality of the students or the quality of the teaching. This violates the tenet of fairness: "In order for an assessment to be fair, all the students should have had the opportunity to learn the material covered in the assessment."

With the advent of standards-based educational reform, the purpose of assessment has shifted considerably. Assessments are used to evaluate how much and how well students have learned the standards during each school year as a result of instruction. This reform is based on what is taught and learned; therefore, teachers must know exactly what standards the students are supposed to learn.

Insights

Of major concern to teachers is that new students arrive unprepared to learn the material being taught at each grade level. Another concern is their lack of knowledge about what content was covered the previous year. If they know a student's previous teacher, they can usually venture a guess as to how prepared or unprepared the student will be. If they don't know a student's previous teacher, they most likely don't have a clue as to preparedness.

One of the most important reasons to have standards is to ensure that students receive a consistent body of knowledge. That way, teachers can capitalize on the information the students already know. They can move forward with new material. If this is not the case, teachers enter into the realm of "PERPETUAL REVIEW."

Barriers to the Implementation of Standards

Many barriers must be overcome in order for a district to implement a standards-based accountability system. In working with the *Illuminati School District Consortium*, we found several barriers to the implementation of standards.

Absence of the Trickle-down Effect. In many districts, the only educators who assert that they have adopted standards are the administrators. Many of the teachers have never heard of their district standards. Somehow the standards have been relegated to compliance issues and have not become part of what the teachers are doing in the classroom.

In other districts, teachers have heard of standards and understand them in a vague way. They may know where to "find" them. They may even know the buzzwords—grade-level standards, proficiencies, benchmarks, exemplars, rubrics, and so on. However, in our experience it is rare for individual teachers to comprehend them in any substantive way or to have assimilated them into the web of daily teaching.

Some districts are making little attempt to utilize standards. Others are trying but find that the misuse of terminology and conflicting explanations and definitions are cause for too much confusion.

Two Major Standards "Myths"

In our discussions with the teachers in the consortium, we discovered what we dubbed **The Two Major Standards Myths**:

• That teachers know what the standards are and they embed them in everything they do.

• That teachers simply cannot teach another thing because they already have too many standards to teach.

Using the California Standards on Language Arts, we created the following grid. We asked teachers to place an X in the areas that they were supposed to be teaching at each grade level.

	K	1	2	3	4	5	6	7	8	9/10	11/12
3. WORD ANALYSIS & SYSTEMATIC VOCABULARY DEVELOPMENT											
Concepts about Print											
Phonemic Awareness											
Decoding and Word Recognition											
Vocabulary and Concept Development											
2. READING COMPREHENSION											
Structural Features of Informational Materials											
Comprehension & Analysis of Grade-Level Appropriate Text											
Expository Critique											
3. LITERACY ANALYSIS & RESPONSE											
Structural Features of Literature											
Narrative Analysis of Grade Level Text											
Literary Criticism											

Without exception, teachers did one of two things: either they filled in every single box, or they filled in boxes that were not part of the content standards for their specific grade levels. After further clarification on our part, some teachers told us that they had no idea where the content standards were "kept."

Guidelines for Implementing a Standards-Based Accountability System

The creation of and the adherence to content standards are very important steps since not only is curriculum "scattered," but so is just about everything related to it. Schools must keep in mind that implementing a standards-based accountability system necessitates a close alignment of content standards to budget, staff development, and evaluation.

The Necessity of Tying Standards to Budget Allocations

Once they have adopted standards for what students should know and be able to do, district personnel must keep in mind that appropriate resources must be allocated. This truism is exemplified in these examples. If a school's language arts content standards require that students perform on-line searches and if students do not have access to computers with that capability, the standard cannot be met. Some science standards require students to perform experiments. If students do not have access to a science lab, they cannot participate in this endeavor. If the history-social science standards require students to conduct investigations using primary source documents, students cannot do so if the library lacks the documents.

Students should not be expected to acquire needed equipment and supplies for themselves. Schools must provide all that is necessary to teach the standards effectively. This is the litmus test which proves or disproves that schools are truly adhering to the spirit of the Opportunity-to-Learn standards.

The Necessity of Tying Standards to Staff Development

When teachers are expected to teach standards and to develop assessments that are aligned with them, they need to be given appropriate tools. When staff development is not pegged to standards, it becomes a series of events with no follow-through or cohesiveness.

In *Brown vs. the Kentucky Department of Education* (discussed in Chapter 1), Brown Middle School had been declared a school in crisis because it fell five points below its goal on the state's accountability index. The state gave this school $14,460 to obtain additional help and assigned two "Distinguished Educators" to help. One of these educators gave a 30-year veteran teacher a very poor evaluation because his lesson was characterized as "disjointed—no connection to what had been previously taught or what will be taught." The teacher contended that he was using "visual math" strategies that he had picked up at a workshop two summers before.

This exemplifies our "culture of fragmentation." The teacher did not know what standards to teach, went to workshops that did not have anything to do with any standards, and taught a lesson without attending to what the students should know in order to move on to the next grade level.

The Necessity of Tying Standards to Administrator and Teacher Evaluations

Schools generate many documents throughout the year, some of which can be used to determine how closely standards are being followed.

- **School-Site Plan.** This document should speak of how teachers are going to be exposed to the new content standards, what type of staff development is planned to enable teachers to teach these standards effectively, and what types of assessments are going to be developed and utilized to make sure that the students are learning the standards well.

87

- **Budget.** Allocation of resources can also be used to see if the materials that are necessary to teach the standards are being purchased. In this age of computers, it might be advisable to add an additional line to specify for which standards the items are being purchased.
- **Report Cards.** These can be changed so that parents are informed about which standards their children are meeting, exceeding, or not meeting.
- **Teacher Grade Book.** These need to be changed so that teachers can keep good records regarding their grading methods and policies and their assignments and assessments which are tied to the standards.
- **Teacher Evaluations.** These can be changed to include the type of content standards teachers will be teaching, how they intend to teach the standards, and the type of assessments they will be developing and utilizing to prove that the students are learning. Teachers can also be asked to keep student work in order to demonstrate that the students are learning the standards.
- **Administrator Evaluations.** Superintendents can align the administrators' evaluations to how well and how fast the schools are implementing the standards. In addition, student achievement in meeting the standards can be included as a measurement of success.

Regarding teacher and administrator evaluation, research has consistently demonstrated that people will try harder in areas in which they are evaluated. Thus, indicators not only measure reality, they change it (Darling-Hammond, 1988).

Insights

Accountability should be based upon descriptions of outcomes, not processes. The question is, "What outcomes should we be responsible for?" The answer is that we should be responsible for outcomes that we can control. Unfortunately, an external norm-referenced test is seldom a genuine indicator of program quality. Rather, it more often indicates characteristics such as the students' prior knowledge, motivation, and the like, which are tied to socio-economic factors.

For example, the following results were obtained by different districts in California, each of which administered the SAT9 test.

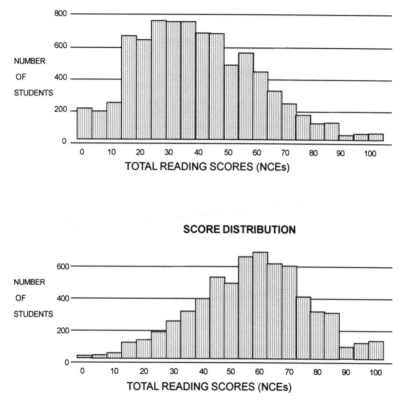

SCORE DISTRIBUTION

NUMBER OF STUDENTS

TOTAL READING SCORES (NCEs)

SCORE DISTRIBUTION

NUMBER OF STUDENTS

TOTAL READING SCORES (NCEs)

In these charts one district has a mean of 56.8 NCEs and the other district has a mean of 38.0 NCEs. Is the instructional program better in the first district and worse in the second district? Is the test truly measuring the quality of the *instructional* program?

COROLLARY:

District and site administrators and teachers should carefully consider the following questions:

- If the test is measuring the quality of the instructional program, shouldn't we fix education by transferring the teachers and administrators in the high-performing schools to the low-performing schools so that the test scores will improve?
- If the test is not measuring the quality of the instructional program, what is the test measuring?
- If the test is measuring quality of the students, should we hold teachers responsible for the demographics of where they happen to be teaching?

The appropriate type of accountability is one which measures the effect teachers have on their students. This is best accomplished by developing and implementing an accountability system that takes into account credible local assessments that truly measure this teacher effect. Assessments must be sensitive to teaching.

Here is another thought-provoking question: the SAT9 is not aligned to the California Standards. If it is not aligned, is the first district in the above example more in alignment with the test than the second district even though nobody knew what the standards were going to be until last year? If this is the case, should we all align to the curriculum of the first district so that we can do well on the test?

The Goal of Implementing Standards

The quality of schools can only be ascertained when they can prove that they have programs in which students are learning the material that is taught in the classrooms. New accountability mandates require that students master specific content at each grade level. This necessitates the adoption of standards that can be used as a blueprint to ensure that ALL students are learning the necessary information and skills. Once there is a clear understanding of what students should learn, effective instructional practices can be designed to teach the standards, and appropriate multiple measures can be developed which are reliable, valid, and fair to ascertain the level at which students are learning the standards.

The standards movement is about assessing "what was taught and what was learned." Educators can no longer be independent contractors with multiple game plans. Standards provide the cohesiveness that will certify the content our students are learning. We must ensure that these are not only adopted in a document for compliance purposes, but that they are understood and adhered to by all of us. In addition, all budgetary staff-development and evaluation practices must coalesce to support their full implementation.

Insights

Many educators will use the term "Standards-Based Education," but few actually understand the term. Standards-based education is a progressing, expanding, non-repeating curriculum of increasing complexity, depth, and breadth. For example, according to the California Mathematics Standards, students in kindergarten should be able to count to 30; in first grade, to 100; in second grade, to 1,000; and so on. In order for students to perform successfully on any assessment which is aligned with standards, they must be presented with the curriculum and instruction for their grade level. Unfortunately, this is not always the case. Many teachers have an informally developed teaching style that evaluates the knowledge of the students during the first days of school and then teaching starts at that level and progresses for 180 days until the end of the term. With this method, the instruction gets more and more behind grade-level each year. In standards-based education the instruction starts at grade-level from the very first day of school each year. Of course, schools can provide extra help for students that are behind, but the core instruction is at grade-level according to standards.

Curriculum Calibration:
What Grade-Level *Are* the Teachers Teaching?

At DataWorks Educational Research, we evaluate student achievement for over 500 California schools each year using multiple measures. We are also involved with eight schools in California's Immediate Intervention/Under Performing Schools Programs. These are schools with sufficiently low scores on the SAT9 norm-reference test that the state determined they needed "immediate intervention" to raise student performance. As part of our investigation of these schools, we went beyond the dissagregations of SAT9 scores and multiple measures. We looked closely at actual examples of day-to-day student work and calibrated each assignment to the California Content Standards. After examining thousands of student papers from the eight schools we discovered an alarming situation: **Instructional materials used at underperforming schools are often well below grade-level, and the higher the grade, the more severe the discrepancy.**

CURRICULUM CALIBRATION:
GRADE-LEVEL OF INSTRUCTIONAL MATERIAL
BEING PRESENTED TO THE STUDENTS

GRADE	PERCENT GRADE-LEVEL STANDARDS						
	K	1	2	3	4	5	Ave.
K	100%						K
1st		100%					1.0
2nd		23	77%				1.8
3rd			45	55%			2.6
4th			40	40	20%		2.8
5th		2	35	59	2	2%	2.7

As can be seen in this example, the curriculum slippage begins in the second grade. By the fifth grade, only two percent of the work being presented to the students is on grade level. An ironic note is that the below-grade level assignments we examined were often stamped with happy faces or graded "A+."

Insights

Upon reviewing Curriculum Calibration results, administrators and teachers alike have expressed first disbelief, then anger and sorrow. However, they quickly moved to the "Aha!" of understanding what "teaching to the standards" really means: All instruction will be on grade-level.

Curriculum calibration provides the missing link to student achievement. We have all looked at standardized test scores, grades, and various multiple-measure results and said, "Now what?" Here is a technique to acquire quantifiable data connecting what goes on in the classroom to assessment results.

COROLLARY:

District and site administrators and **teachers** should understand that it is difficult to raise test scores when students are receiving instruction that is below grade-level. Schools should:

- Adopt a policy that all instruction will be at grade-level according to standards.
- Identify the grade-level of materials being used. For example, "GLS K," "GLS 1," etc. so teachers will use correct materials at each grade.
- At least twice per year, perform a curriculum calibration to see where each school and grade stands.
- Redirect school training and resources to reach grade-level teaching.

7

DATA-DRIVEN
SCHOOL
IMPROVEMENT

Beyond Compliance

Central to the latest direction in school reform are two intertwining elements:

- Standards that clearly define what students should learn as a result of schooling
- Multiple measure accountability systems that inform schools how successfully students are meeting the standards

An outgrowth of the first element has been the creation of a plethora of materials related to standards, and that of the second element has been the generation of huge quantities of data. Arising from these situations are two very important questions:

- What should be done with all this information?
- How can districts use data to transcend mere compliance and substantially improve their students' academic achievement?

Traditionally, districts have used data for compliance reporting. Usually data is collected for the sole purpose of completing a report for submission to a state or federal agency. Johnson states, "We do the testing, and we get the individual student's scores back, but there's no concerted effort to interpret the data and work with [it]" (1996).

We are not arguing against the use of data to prove compliance. We do, however, recommend using data for two additional purposes which are more powerful since they are proactive rather than reactive:

- to improve student achievement
- to enhance accountability at all levels

Over the past six years, more and more educators have written about the importance of data collection and its use as a means of improving academic achievement. McLean, for example, contends that data collection and use has an impact on educational improvement without parallel (1996).

What we need is a dynamic, data-driven accountability system which is used by administrators and teachers throughout the year. The following insights gained in our work with the consortium are the backbone of such a system.

Insights

In order to create a dynamic accountability system, the following steps should be taken:

1. Develop a process that involves teachers, administrators, students, parents, and other community members.
2. Establish desirable content standards for each discipline.
3. At the district, school, and classroom level, develop valid, reliable, and fair performance standards (multiple measures) which assess how well the students have learned the content standards.
4. Disaggregate data by school, grade, federal and state compensatory programs (Title I, Special Education, Migrant, LEP, Gifted and Talented), ethnicity, gender, and socio-economic level to determine the quality and equity of the educational process.
5. Provide a process for analyzing the data to identify the variables related to program successes and weaknesses.
6. Write an action plan to improve the achievement of students who do not meet the standards.
7. Communicate the results to members of the school community and to the public.
8. Monitor the program throughout the year and keep teachers informed as to how well they are meeting the goals of the action plan.

District and site administrators and teachers should keep the following in mind:

- Make sure that the action plan is based on value-added gains and not in absolutes because classes might not be equally distributed. For example, a teacher might start out a year with 20% of the students able to read, whereas another teacher might start out with 80% of the students able to read. The expectations for teachers should be improvement from where their students are at the beginning of the year.

- Make sure that the action plan is based on outcomes and not on processes.

Processes	Outcomes
How many books are in the library?	How many students can read?
How many computers are in the school?	How many reports are completed by means of technology?
How much homework is assigned?	How many students passed the test?

Accountability at Different Levels

Data is only helpful when it is generated at different levels so that the educators responsible for student achievement can be properly evaluated and assisted. We recommend disaggregating data according to three levels: by school, by grade, and by individual student.

Accountability at the School Level

So that superintendents can evaluate individual schools as well as the district as a whole, data should be disaggregated at the school level. The data on the next page shows the results of a multiple measures analysis for students meeting mathematics grade-level standards by school. There is both a table and graphical presentation of the data.

Accountability at the School Level

ILLUMINATI SCHOOL DISTRICT CONSORTIUM

SCHOOL		MATHEMATICS GRADE-LEVEL STANDARDS			
		DO NOT MEET	MEET	EXCEED	TOTAL
LOWER ELEMENTARY	Count	229	305	118	652
	%	35.1%	46.8%	18.1%	100.0%
UPPER ELEMENTARY	Count	252	286	108	646
	%	39.0%	44.3%	16.7%	100.0%
MIDDLE SCHOOL	Count	266	228	180	674
	%	39.5%	33.8%	26.7%	100.0%
TOTAL	Count	747	819	406	1972
	%	37.9%	41.5%	20.6%	100.0%

MATHEMATICS GRADE-LEVEL STANDARDS

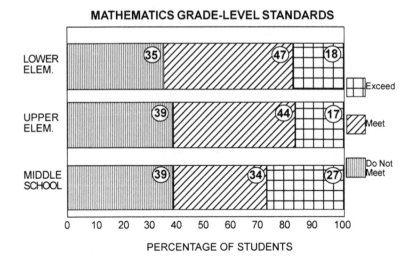

PERCENTAGE OF STUDENTS

High-Stakes Decisions and Multiple Measures

During the last two years, districts across the nation are stressing the importance of accountability as a means for high-stakes decision making for schools, administrators, teachers, and individual students.

- If schools fail to meet certain growth targets, the government might take over the school, reassign teachers and principals, and allow parents to select the school of their choice.
- If individual students fail to pass a high school exit exam, they can be denied a diploma.
- If students fail to meet grade-level standards, they can be retained.

Multiple measures is the only way to ensure that schools, teachers, and students are not penalized based on one end-of-the-year norm-referenced test that does not measure all the outcomes of education.

Accountability at the Grade Level

Data disaggregated at the grade level for each school will help the principal and teachers determine which groups are having the most difficulty and in which areas. Teachers can then meet by grade level to plan necessary interventions.

During the analysis of the students' mathematics grade-level standards results shown on the next page, questions in two general areas will arise:

- Are the assessments accurate for each grade level?
- If so, why are all students not equally successful?
  Further analysis leads to further queries:
- Are standards well-articulated for each grade?
- Are enough resources being allocated where needed?
- Is staff development adequate and connected to the standards?
- Are the successes of kindergartners and first graders fading by third or fourth grade? If so, why?
- Are rubrics consistent for each grade level?

Accountability at the Grade Level

ILLUMINATI SCHOOL DISTRICT CONSORTIUM

GRADE		MATHEMATICS GRADE-LEVEL STANDARDS			TOTAL
		DO NOT MEET	MEET	EXCEED	
K	Count	65	107	43	215
	%	30.2%	49.8%	20.0%	100.0%
1	Count	59	139	22	220
	%	26.8%	63.2%	10.0%	100.0%
2	Count	104	59	53	216
	%	48.1%	27.3%	24.5%	100.0%
3	Count	69	109	49	227
	%	30.5%	48.0%	21.6%	100.0%
4	Count	100	98	27	225
	%	44.4%	43.6%	12.0%	100.0%
5	Count	83	79	32	194
	%	42.8%	40.7%	16.5%	100.0%
6	Count	84	58	77	219
	%	38.4%	26.5%	35.2%	100.0%
7	Count	116	55	67	238
	%	48.7%	23.1%	28.2%	100.0%
8	Count	66	115	36	217
	%	30.4%	53.0%	16.6%	100.0%
TOTAL	Count	746	819	406	1971
	%	37.8%	41.6%	20.6%	100.0%

MATHEMATICS GRADE-LEVEL STANDARDS

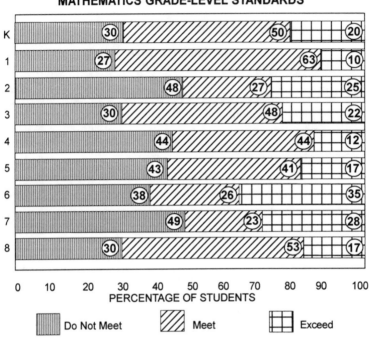

PERCENTAGE OF STUDENTS

Do Not Meet · Meet · Exceed

Insights #1

Comparing grades requires thoughtful consideration. K and 1 usually don't include a norm-referenced test and tend to show higher
results. Also, grades 2 through 6 might have one set of assessments and grades 7 and 8 at a middle school probably used a
different set. As districts gain experience, their assessments become more accurately calibrated can be better used to compare
between grades.

Insights #2

Districts and schools have to be very careful analyzing data where
student achievement might not be equally distributed at the different sites; therefore, ensure that schools are judged for their ability
to improve (value-added gains) as opposed to absolute scores.
Another caution with data analysis is that conclusions cannot be
made based on one year's results. There is too much statistical
fluctuation to base decisions on the results of one year. It is important to analyze data over at least three years.

Accountability at the Individual Student Level

In addition to the district level and school level data, results also need to be presented for each individual student.

INDIVIDUAL STUDENTS
*GLS=Grade-Level Standards: Does Not Meet (DNM), Meets, or Exceeds

ID	Name	Lang Grade	SAT9 NP Lang	READ/LANG GLS*	Math Grade	SAT9 NP Math	MATH GLS*	Title I	Migrant	LEP	RSP	GATE
111	Farrow, Dontay	C	60	MEETS	A	43	EXCEEDS					X
222	Huerta, Jorge	A	54	EXCEEDS	C	87	EXCEEDS			X		
333	Smith, Kelly	D	18	DNM	B	68	MEETS	X				
444	Wright, Sarah	C	90	EXCEEDS	D	18	DNM					
555	Quezada, Sofia	B	62	EXCEEDS	C	52	MEETS		X			
666	Romsey, Jack	C	42	MEETS	C	48	MEETS					
777	Tagay, Jordan	C	22	DNM	F	52	DNM				X	
888	Lee, Yasmine	A	88	EXCEEDS	A	92	EXCEEDS			X		
999	Outten, Krist	D	99	EXCEEDS	A	32	MEETS					X
101010	Restrepo, Sam	B	57	EXCEEDS	C	91	EXCEEDS					

Individual accountability gives valuable information about each student. From the table we can surmise the following:

- Student 111 is a GATE student who is exceeding grade-level standards in math by only meeting grade-level standards in language-arts.
- Student 222 is an LEP student who is exceeding at everything. This student can be recommended for grants or scholarships.
- Student 333 is a Title I student who needs to be remediated in Language only.
- Student 555 is a migrant student who is exceeding language grade-level standards and meeting mathematics grade-level standards.
- Student 999 is a GATE student who is doing very well in norm-referenced tests but not very well in his Language class.

Measuring Improvement Over Time

It cannot be concluded from one year that one school is doing better than the other. In two years, all we have are comparisons of two years. Not until the third year can conclusions be drawn regarding these questions: Are the schools actually improving? How significant are the statistical fluctuations? For this example, it is school C that showed the most improvement over the years.

RESULTS OF WRITING SAMPLE
Number of Students Meeting
Grade-Level Standards

School	Year 1	Year 2	Year 3
A	48%	58%	50%
B	63%	60%	67%
C	35%	40%	48%

COROLLARY:
District and site administrators and teachers must be sure the following are true:

- Data should be seen in the context of each school site, classroom, or individual students. Improvement should always be measured as value-added gains and not in absolutes.
- Before we make conclusions about how well-schools are doing, there has to be at least three years of collected data to determine if there is a trend or if the changes are merely due to statistical fluctuations.

The term "assessment" is often used in different contexts, and it means different things to different people. Most educators think of assessment in terms of testing and grading, scoring quizzes and exams, and assigning report card grades. In contrast, the emerging vision of assessment is that of a dynamic process that continuously yields information about student progress toward the achievement of learning goals.

The interpretation of assessment as a dynamic process acknowledges that when the information gathered is consistent with learning goals and is used appropriately to focus instruction, it can enhance student learning as well as document it (Mathematical Sciences Education Board, 1993).

Rather than being an activity which is separate from instruction, assessment is thus viewed as an integral part of teaching and learning, and not just the culmination of instruction (Mathematical Sciences Education Board, 1993). When educators are informed of their students' learning progress, better decisions can be made about how to teach in a manner that will maximize the students' learning (Fuchs, 1995).

Data Interpretation

Looking at Data that Compare Groups

When different groups are compared, districts should also look at actual numbers of students that were tested to see if it is a representative sample for all groups. For example, in a school with 2,000 white students and only four American Indians, generalities cannot be made about the American Indian group since the sample is so small.

Comparing the Results of Several Measures

Charts that compare the results of each of several measures often show large disparities. These differences may be due to one or more of several factors:

- The quality of one or more tests is poor.
- One test ranks students while the other measures the students' content knowledge.
- One test is mis-calibrated, with cut-off points set too high or too low.
- The tests do not measure the same content area.

It must be remembered that norm-referenced tests are designed to rank students into a bell curve. This means that students are compared to each other in a continuum from 1 through 99 and that 50% of the students by definition will always fall above 50 and 50% will always fall below 50. Any improvements in overall scores are removed to maintain the bell curve centered on the 50th percentile. On the other hand, criterion-referenced tests are graded against a standard, which makes it possible for all students to attain the grade-level standard if they learn the material.

The Emerging Vision of Accountability

Traditional Practices
- Only one single external measure is used.
- The test is given once a year.
- Short-answer and multiple-choice items predominate.
- Testing is used to rank students.

Transitional Practices
- More than one measure is used.
- Some measures are still in the process of being developed.
- Assessment is beginning to be aligned with curriculum and instruction.

Desired Practices
- Multiple measures are used.
- Testing and teaching arealigned to content standards.
- Everyone has the same opportunity to learn the material.
- Student progress is continuously monitored to redirect teaching.

From a Single Measure to Multiple Measures

This book has presented a case for the use of multiple measures to assess student learning. Before concluding, we must underscore two points made previously:

- We are not advocating the use of multiple measures in an attempt to manipulate data so that under-achieving students will appear to be doing better than they are.
- We are advocating a more accurate measure of what students have actually learned in the classroom.

Multiple measures can be used as part of an overall program of measuring and improving student learning when we adhere to the following precepts:

- Embrace standards.
- Make sure that schools develop the capacity to teach to the standards.
- Develop measures that are in alignment with content standards.
- Measure student progress.

- Analyze results to see if school interventions have succeeded in increasing student achievement.
- Adjust the educational processes if necessary.

One more point which we must emphasize is that we are not advocating the abolishment of norm-referenced tests. On the contrary, we suggest that educators develop a better understanding of the uses and limitations of testing, keeping in mind that when we test students, we are trying to determine the answers to these questions:

- Have schools been successful in their mission to educate students?
- Have students attained the knowledge and skill to be successful in the next step of their lives, whether as a student or worker?

With the use of multiple measures, student evaluations will be more accurate because of the following factors:

- The standard error of measurement, inherent in any test, is reduced.
- No single measure can assess all the content standards that we want our students to know and be able to do.
- Other measures are included that measure what students have learned as opposed to how they rank with each other.

As we work to implement standards and to assess the success of students in meeting them, let us remember the multiple measure imperative:

USING MORE THAN ONE MEASURE GIVES US MULTIPLE WAYS OF "SEEING" STUDENT ACHIEVEMENT AND ALLOWS US TO CERTIFY STUDENT LEARNING ACCURATELY.

The use of multiple measures is the only fair way to assess learning. We owe it to our students. Let's start developing the various measures now!

REFERENCES

Archives, E. P. (1996, November). *What does the psychometrician's classroom look like?: Reframing assessment concepts in the context of learning* [On-line]. http://olam.ed.asu.edu/epaa/v4n17.html

Astin, A. W. (1982). *Excellence and equity in American education.* Washington, DC: National Commission on Excellence in Education.

Austin, S. &. McCann, R. (1992, April 23). *Here's another arbitrary grade for your collection: A statewide study of grading policies.* San Francisco: American Educational Research Association, Research for Better Schools, Inc.

Bachman, L. F. (1990). Assessment and evaluation. *Annual Review of Applied Linguistics.* USA: Cambridge UP, 210-226.

Borman, G. D. &. D'Agostino, J. V. (1996, Winter). Title I and student achievement: A meta-analysis of federal evaluation results. *Educational Evaluation and Policy Analysis, 18*(4): 309-326.

Brandt, R. (1992). On performance assessment: A conversation with Grant Wiggins. *Educational Leadership, 49*(8): 35-37.

Burden, P. R. (Ed). (1993). Addressing the national goals. *Journal of Staff Development, 14* (4), i.

Burrill, L. E. (undated). How a Standardized Achievement Test is Built. *Test Service Notebook 125.* The Psychological Corporation.

Campbell-Hill, B. & Ruptic, C. A. (1994). *Practical aspects authentic assessment: Putting the pieces together.* Norwood, MA: Christopher-Gordon Publishers, Inc.

Commission On Chapter I. (1993, January 13). Making schools work for children in poverty. *Education Week,* 46-48.

Coordinated Compliance Review. (1997, Fall). *Standards-based assessment and accountability system for coordinated compliance review [CCR].* Sacramento: California State Department of Education.

Council of Chief State School Officers (1992). Summary of recommendations and policy implications for improving the assessment and monitoring of students with limited English proficiency [On-line]. http:/www.ccsso.org/leppol.htlm

Cross, L. H. & Frary R. B. (1996, April). Hodgepodge grading: Endorsed by students and teachers alike. New York: National Council on Measurement in Education. Virginia Polytechnic Institute and State University. *Educational Leadership and Policy Studies.*

Cziko, G. A. (1987). Review of the bilingual syntax measure. In J. C. Alderson, K. J. Krahnke, & C. W. Starsfield, *Reviews of English language proficiency tests.* Washington, DC: Teachers of English to Speakers of Other Languages.

Darling-Hammond, L. (1983, Fall). Teacher evaluation in the organization context: A review of the literature. *Review of Educational Research, 53*(3): 285-328.

Darling-Hammond, L. (1988, June). *Assessment and incentives: The medium is the message.* Chicago: Association of Assessment in Higher Education, Third National Conference on Assessment in Higher Education.

Education Research Report. (1992, November). Parental satisfaction with schools and the need for standards. *Education Research Report* ED 352-206.

Elliot, J. et al. (1997). *Providing assessment accommodations for students with disabilities in state and district assessments.* National Center on Educational Outcomes Policy Directions, Number 7 [On-line]. http://www.coled.umn.edu/NCEO/OnlinePubs/Policy7.html.

Feinberg, L. (1990). Multiple-choice and its critics. *College Board Review* 156: 12-17.

Fuchs, L. S. (1995, June). *Connecting performance assessment to instruction: A comparison of behavioral assessment, mastery learning, curriculum-based measurement, and performance assessment.* ERIC Document Reproduction Service No. ED 381 984.

Gillmore, G. & Dickerson, A. (1979). *The Relationship Between Instruments Used for Identifying Children of Limited English-speaking Ability in Texas.* Arlington, VA: Education Resources.

Haber, L. (Ed.) (1985). Review of language assessment scales. In *The Ninth Mental Measurements Yearbook.* Lincoln, NE: Burros Institute of Mental Measurements & the University of Nebraska.

Harp, B. (1996). *The handbook of literacy assessment and evaluation.* Norwood, MA: Christopher-Gordon Publishers, Inc.

Herman, J. L., Aschbacher, P. R., & Winters, L. (1992). *A practical guide to alternative assessment.* Alexandria, VA: Association of Supervision and Curriculum Development.

Hibbard, M. K., Van Wagener, L., Lewbel, S., Waterbury-Wyatt, S., & Shaw, S. (1996). *A teacher's guide to performance-based learning and assessment.* Alexandria, VA: Association of Supervision and Curriculum Development.

Hieronymus, A. N. & Hoover, H. D. (1987). *Iowa tests of basic skills writing supplement teacher's guide.* Chicago: Riverside Publishing Company.

Hills, T. W. (1997). *Critical issue: Assessing young children's progress appropriately* [On-line]. http://www.ncrel.org/sdrs/areas/issues/students/earlycld/ea500.htm

Holland, H. (1997, October). *Brown vs. the Department of Education.* Louisville Magazine/Web Edition [On-line]. http://louisville.com/loumag/oct97/brown.htlm

Hopstock, P. J., Bucaro, B. J., Fleischman, H. I., Zehler, A. M., & Eu, H. (1993). *Descriptive study of services to limited English proficient students.* Arlington, VA: Development Associates, Inc. Report to the U. S. Department of Education, Office of Policy and Planning, Volume II: Survey Results.

Johnson, J. H. (1996, May). *Data-driven school improvement.* Eugene, OR: Oregon School Study Council.

Lawton, M. (1995, December 13). *Education, civil-rights coalition backs task-based assessments.* Education Week.

Lawton, M. (1997, October 22). *State boards' leaders call for assessments bearing consequences.* Education Week.

LaCelle-Peterson, M. & Rivera, C. (1994). Is it real for all kids? A framework for equitable assessment policies for English language learners. *Harvard Educational Review, 64*(1): 55-75.

McCollum, P. A. (1987). *Theories of second language learning.* London: Edward Arnold.

McLean, J. E. (1996). *Improving education through action research: A guide for administrators and teachers.* Thousand Oaks, CA: Corwin Press ED 380-884.

Marzano, R. J., Pickering, D., & McTighe, J. (1993). *Assessing student outcomes.* Alexandria, VA: Association for Supervision and Curriculum Development.

107

Mathematical Sciences Education Board. (1993). *Measuring what counts: A conceptual guide for mathematical assessment.* Washington, DC: National Academy Press.

Opportunity-to-Learn Standards. (1995). *NCEO policy directions.* Minneapolis, MN: University of Minnesota. Pub. National Center on Educational Outcomes. NCEO—Policy Directions/Issue 4, January, 1995, (p. 1) [On-line]. http://www.coled.umn.edu/NCEO/OnlinePubs/Policy4.html

Newmann, F. M. & King, M. B. (1997, Spring). Accountability and school performance: Implications from restructuring schools. *Harvard Educational Review, 67* (1).

Oller, J. (1992). *Language testing research: Lessons applied to LEP students and programs.* Proceedings of the Second National Research Symposium on Limited English Proficient Student Issues: Focus on Evaluation and Measurement. Washington, DC: U. S. Department of Education, Office of Bilingual Education and Minority Languages Affairs. Volume 2.

Parsons, T. (1959). The school class as a social system: Some of its functions in American society. *Harvard Educational Review, 29*: 297-318.

Prince, S. B. & Taylor, R. G. (1995). Should the correlates of effective schools be used as a prescription for improving achievement? *Educational Research Quarterly, 18*(4): 19-26.

Rothman, R. (1995). *Measuring up: Standards, assessment and school reform.* San Francisco: Jossey-Bass.

Secada, W. (1994). *Issues in the development of Spanish-language versions of the national assessment of educational progress.* Stanford, CA: The National Academy of Education.

Shavelson, R. (1997). The splintered curriculum. *Education Week.*

Shavelson, R. J. & Baxter, G. P. (1992, May). What we've learned about assessing hands-on science. *Educational Leadership,* 20-25.

Staff (1997). *Fair test fact sheet: The SAT.* [On-line]. http://www.fairtest.org/facts/satfact.htm

Supovitz, J. A. & Brennan, R. T. (1997). Mirror, mirror on the wall, which is the fairest test of all? *Harvard Educational Review, 67*(3): 472-505.

Tannenbaum, J. (1996). *Practical ideas on alternative assessment for ESL students.* ERIC Clearinghouse on Languages and Linguistics ED395500.

University of California. (1996). *Introducing the University: 1997-98.*

U. S. Congress, (1992). *Testing in America's schools: Asking the right questions* (OTA-SET-519). Washington, DC: U. S. Government Printing Office.

Welsh, P. (Spring 1992). It takes two to tango. *American Educator, 16*(1): 18-23.

Wiggins, G. (1993, November). Assessment, authenticity, content, and validity. *Phi Delta Kappan.*

Ysseldyke, J., et al. (1994). *Students with disabilities and educational standards: Recommendations for policy and practice.* National Center on Educational Outcomes, Policy Direction, Number 2.

Zehler, A. M., Hopstock, P. J., Fleischman, H. L., & Greniuk, C. A. (1994). *An examination of assessment of limited English proficient students.* Task Order D070 Report [On-line]. http://www.ncbe.gwu.edu/miscpubs/siac/lepasses.html

Zigarelli, M. A. (1996, November/December). An empirical test of conclusions from effective school research. *The Journal of Educational Research 90*(2): 103-108.

Index

Students in alternative systems, assessing
   achievement of, 59, 67-68
   relevant domains of learning, 67-68
Students with disabilities, assessing
   achievement of, 59, 65-67
   accommodations for, 65-66
   history of, 65
Student work, teacher evaluation of, 41.
      See also Checklists; Grades; Port-
      folios; Running records
Supovitz, J. A., 8, 9, 12

Tannenbaum, J., 74
Taylor, R. G., 4
Teacher evaluations, 88
Teacher grade book, 88
Teacher morale, 15
Test activities, 18, 19, 22, 23
   complex, 18, 19, 22
   simple, 18, 19, 22
Test bias, 9, 13, 35
Test content, 18, 20
   contextualized, 18, 20
   decontextualized, 18, 20
Test fairness, 23, 24, 35-39, 40, 83
Test knowledge, 18, 20, 22
   authentic, 18, 20, 22
   contrived, 18, 20, 22
Test questions, 18, 19, 21, 23
   objective, 18, 19, 21
   subjective, 18, 19, 22
Test raters:
   judgment of, 38
   standardization of, 27
   See also Rater reliability
Test reliability, 23, 24-30, 38, 39, 40, 83
   checklist, 27
   conditions supporting, 27-30
   observed score, 24
   true score, 24
   See also Error of measurement
Tests, 28

differences in, 18-23
standardization of, 17-18
See also specific types of tests; Test ac-
   tivities; Test content; Test knowl-
   edge; Test questions; Test tasks
Test scores, disaggregating, 51
Test-taking atmosphere, 9
Test tasks, 18, 20, 22
   meaningful, 18, 20, 22
   trivial, 18, 20, 22
Test validity, 23, 24, 30-35, 38, 39, 40, 83.
   See also specific types of validity
Third International Mathematics and Sci-
   ence Study (TIMSS), 82
Title I, 41, 95
   students, 46, 47, 51, 54, 55-57
Tracking students, 10, 51
True-false questions, 19

U. S. Congress, 18
United States Constitution Test, 17
University of California, 33

Validity. *See* Test validity
Van Wagener, L., 64

Waterbury-Wyatt, S., 64
Welsh, P., 82
Wiggins, G., 26, 58
Winters, L., 27
Writing samples, 41, 47
Writing skills, measurement of, 7

Ysseldyke, J., 65

Zehler, A. M., 64
Zigarelli, M. A., 4

114